Published by the University of Warw

ISBN 0 902683 14 4

Table of Contents

Vice-Chancellor's Foreword

As a relative newcomer to the University (five years' service rather than twenty-five), I have spent some time reflecting upon the reasons for its success. This book confirms my own conclusion that the University was founded on a very clear set of guiding principles to which it has adhered throughout its development. Put very simply, these principles comprise a commitment to take on only those activities which can be done properly, to ensure that the leaders of such activities are given the freedom to develop them effectively without too many rules and too much bureaucracy, and to retain flexibility and the ability to respond as opportunities arise to enhance academic excellence.

This book has been carefully prepared, using both archival material and the memories of some of those directly involved. It makes an appropriate permanent memento to mark the celebration of the first twenty-five years. I am grateful to all who helped to produce it, most particularly, of course, to Michael Shattock, and to Bob Burgess. I am sure all who have an interest in the University of Warwick will find it fascinating to read.

Dr C. L. Brundin
Vice-Chancellor

Making a University

"The true act of foundation is a process, and it coincides with no single point of time: it lies embedded in the activities of the men to whose energy, whose generosity of time and money, whose fruitful vision we owe the planning and construction of our University scheme."

Lord Radcliffe, 1 July 1967[1]

The founders of the English New Universities – East Anglia, Essex, Kent, Lancaster, Sussex, Warwick and York – perhaps not surprisingly believed that each of their universities was going to make an immediate impact on the national and international university scene. One, rather incautiously, delivered his prospectus for the future in the form of the Reith Lectures, and began by saying: "It may seem odd that I should begin this series of lectures with the claim that the University . . . is going to be big, as though bigness were important. I believe it is important"[2]. Twenty-seven years later the university had only reached 3,500 student numbers instead of the 10,000 or even 20,000 that were then envisaged. Of course part of the problem that all the New Universities faced was that the early promises of generous funding from the University Grants Committee were soon forgotten and, as the university system as a whole stumbled through the sudden suspension of the building programme in 1973-4, the high inflation of the later 1970s and the cuts of the 1980s, the New Universities' struggles to achieve 'critical mass' were given low priority.

Warwick is now the largest of the New Universities in terms of student numbers – around 8,000 as against 5,000 in the next largest. It is also, according to the public record, the most successful. This success reflects the principles on which the University was founded and the style, personality or way of doing things which has evolved from the patterns that were set in the first years. We can agree with Cardinal Newman when he says that:

> To set on foot and to maintain in life and vigour a real University is . . . one of those greatest works, great in their difficulty and their importance, on which we deservedly expended the rarest intellects and the most varied endowments.[3]

But what is evident from Warwick's history is that creating a university community and bringing it to a sufficient size and level of academic distinction that it can make a real impact locally, nationally and internationally is a lengthy process. In celebrating its Twenty-Fifth Anniversary the University is also celebrating the fact that it has reached a maturity when the long period of formation, of making the University, is at an end. Its academic departments and programmes are firmly established and a high proportion of its staff have built their careers here, the shape of its campus has assumed an appearance of permanence and it has a significant number of graduates – over 30,000 – now working in the wider community. The University is also at a point when it can face the 1990s and the years beyond 2000 with confidence: it can launch the new initiatives which social and other changes will demand from a secure base and it retains the flexibility and vigour to make them a success. It is, in fact, poised for new developments.

This volume does not attempt to be a history of the University. If there is ever a time when such a book should be written it is a task for someone who has not been an active participant in the events to be described. What it does seek to do is to give a sense of the University's history through descriptions of its origins and its academic roots and through a pictorial account of the past twenty-five years.

Acknowledgements

There have been many contributors to the volume. First let me record my gratitude to Bob Burgess, Professor of Sociology and Director of the Centre for Educational Development, Appraisal and Research, for taking time away from so many other commitments to research and write the chapter on the principles on which the academic development of the University was based. Within the Senate House thanks go variously to Geoffrey Middleton, Peter Dunn, Collin Ferguson (who technically is not in the Senate House), Sally Roper and to my secretary, Karen Stewart. Particular thanks must go to Dr Roberta Warman for creating the University's photographic archive, for her patience in helping me to put the pictorial account together, and for piloting the volume as a whole through the printers. I must also pay tribute to the designer, Stuart Clitherow of Petrel and Porpoise Design, and to Kathy Gledhill who in 1986-7 assisted me in setting up a University of Warwick Archive which was an essential preliminary to the preparation of the volume.

Finally my thanks must go to the Universities Funding Council for giving me special access to UGC records, still embargoed by the 30 years rule, in the Public Record Office, to the staff of the Coventry Record Office for their helpfulness, to Henry Rees for depositing his papers about the University for consultation in the Archive, to Helene Barratt (herself a Warwick graduate) for allowing me to consult her father's unpublished diaries, and to the staff of the *Coventry Evening Telegraph* for their ready assistance in tracking down pictures. My warm appreciation, as always, goes to my colleagues for their encouragement in the project.

Michael Shattock

The Pre-history of the University

Michael Shattock

When the new University of Warwick's first staff took up their appointments on what was literally a green field site in 1963 and 1964, they were so occupied in the myriad of tasks required to prepare for the first intake of undergraduates in October 1965 they had no time and little inclination to reflect on how the University came there, who had campaigned for it and why. Yet the University's pre-history is of considerable interest because of the extent to which it reflects the forces at work locally in Coventry and Warwickshire to found a university and the light it casts on the interplay between local initiative and national policy in the development of higher education in the post-war period. It is also important because the pre-history had a profound impact on the structure, constitution and academic programme of the University in a way that very few of its first staff or students ever appreciated. This pre-history is unique among the New Universities because of the political and industrial make-up of the region and because of the differences in educational philosophy which had to be resolved before the University could be launched.

The first ideas about a university

The first spokesman for the concept of a university in Coventry was Dr Neville Gorton, Bishop of Coventry from 1942 to his death in 1955. Gorton was an unusual bishop and an unusual man. Educated at Marlborough and Balliol College, Oxford, he came to the bishopric from the headmastership of Blundells School. From this slightly unpropitious background for a ministry in the industrial West Midlands he revolutionised the relationship between the church and the two sides of industry in Coventry, invented the idea of an industrial chaplaincy and formed close personal friendships with municipal leaders. In particular he had a vision of the inter-relationship which should exist between industry in the West Midlands and higher education.

He launched the University idea in March 1943 at a civic function to welcome him to Coventry when he said that Coventry was the ideal location for a University of Technology and that he intended to embark on discussions with trades unionists and employers to see how it could be brought about. The *Coventry Evening Telegraph* records that his speech made 'a tremendous impression'.[1] Later in the year he wrote a paper 'Claim for a Technological University in Coventry' in which he put forward two basic arguments. The first was that the country suffered from a separation of science from industry and that a university, and particularly university professorships, would attract first class scientists to Coventry who would work on industrial problems and attract outstanding students to work in local companies. A complementary function of the university should be to offer adult education classes for the workforce and courses for trades unionists. The second was cultural:

You have a town of immense importance in the industry of this country. But it is a danger centre. It has no unity of life. It has no cultural interests – no people to create them. It lacks an intellectual centre and leadership. Give it a university and the university will not only feed itself but feed Coventry and give it life and direction and self-consciousness.[2]

But there were too many other more pressing problems both locally and nationally to make much progress on the realisation of these ideas during the war years, not least for Gorton, his plan to rebuild the Cathedral.

By 1945 consideration was actively being given nationally to the future size and shape of the university system. The two forces which drove the review were Britain's need for scientific manpower and the pressure of demand for places for ex-servicemen. In April of that year two of its members, Professor R. H. Tawney and Sir Henry Tizard, put strong pressure on the University Grants Committee (UGC) in a paper which argued that since the existing universities could not meet the expansion targets which the nation required some new residential universities might need to be founded.[3] Their argument was not, however, well received by the Treasury which regarded the economic position of the country as rendering any thought of wholly new university foundations to be out of the question. The UGC turned down Lampeter College's bid to be placed on the UGC grant list though it accepted the claims of the University Colleges of Hull and Leicester which had been held over from the immediate pre-war years. But publication of the Barlow Report on Scientific Manpower in 1946[4], which recommended an expansion of training in science and technology, led to an upsurge of interest in various parts of the country. The UGC received delegations from Bradford, Brighton, Norwich, Stoke and York but only the proposed University College of North Staffordshire at Stoke (later to become Keele University) was permitted to go forward, even though it was not technological, because of Tawney's advocacy within the UGC and the Labour Government's special sympathy for Stoke's case. In supporting Stoke the Government overrode the objections of the Committee of Vice-Chancellors and Principals (CVCP) which supported the UGC's reluctance to found new institutions on the grounds that scarce resources were better directed to existing universities.

The Barlow Report had proposed that Britain needed a new technological university along the lines of the Massachussets Institute of Technology (MIT) or the California Institute of Technology (Cal Tech). This proposal was to reappear at regular intervals in the next few years as the linkage between national economic performance and technological shortfall became more explicit in the public mind. Gorton's advocacy and Coventry's importance as an engineering centre made it a natural focus for some of these discussions and the *Financial Times* carried a leader in December 1951 which argued the case for a British MIT and went on to ask:

> Where should a new British technological university be placed? Obviously at Coventry which would greatly benefit by the existence of an institution for the promotion of education in the higher branches of learning. That City might be described as the mechanical centre of England . . . Could any better use be made of the wealth accumulated by some of the heads of British engineering and motor businesses than the endowment of a new technological university.[5]

The question was also debated in the Parliamentary and Scientific Committee, a non-party committee composed of members of both Houses of Parliament and representatives of science and industry, which became a powerful pressure group for the expansion of technological education. The Committee's interest stimulated debates in the House of Lords in 1952 and 1954. Gorton spoke in the first of these and joined the Committee soon afterwards. In his speech he described how in the previous five months he had visited 20 to 25 factories and had discussed the university idea extensively with trades unionists. Coventry was 'the last word in modern industry'; Whittle had been trained in Coventry (not of course at a university★) and Coventry had 'any number of potential Whittles if it is given the opportunity of eliciting them'. Coventry had an

> interlocking unity on the engineering side: light subsidiary engineering, tool machines on a very big scale, the motor of every type and the aeroplane – an independent unit in the use of steel and light metal alloy. It is a centre where one can see scientific research being deployed on one overall related problem, and see the direct application of technology, the whole of Coventry's engineering being a single research area on one group of problems which can be isolated and therefore scientifically handled . . . The whole working industry at your door, in its human management and trades union setting, as well as in its technological problems, forms your research laboratory.[6]

The speech drew no immediate response in Coventry but in December 1953 the *Coventry Evening Standard* carried a leader entitled 'Why not a University for Coventry?'. The leader had initially been drafted as an article to start a debate about university education in Coventry by Henry Rees, then a Lecturer in Geography at the Coventry Technical College. It argued, unlike Gorton, that such a university should not be exclusively technological but a 'complete institution of advanced learning'.[7] The leader stimulated a considerable and on the whole warmly supportive range of letters from the three Coventry MPs, Crossman, Edelman and Burton, from the Labour Parliamentary candidate for Stratford, T. L. K. Locksley, and from members of the public including Kenneth Richardson, a colleague of Rees at the College, and Walter Chinn, the Director of Education for Coventry, writing in a personal capacity. Disagreement, however, came from the Principal of the Technical College, H. V. Field, who argued that student demand would be insufficient to justify a university and that the costs, which would be high, would have to be borne by the local authority.[8] Another view, which was to re-surface many times in the next few years, suggested that Coventry should concentrate its energies on lower level technical education.

Interest in the idea, which was further fanned by two signed articles by Rees on the history of the founding of Birmingham University[9], was such that in April 1954 the Lord Mayor was persuaded to call a meeting of interested persons. Discussion there illustrated many subsequent themes in the debate about what kind of university was needed in Coventry[10]. Gorton could not be present but his view that what Coventry as an engineering city needed was 'a marriage between industry and technology on the one hand and academic knowledge on the other', was presented by the Provost. Councillor E. A. C. Roberts on the other hand wanted to see a more broadly based institution. But there were significant voices against the whole proposal including Field and W. A. Weaver of the Coventry Chamber of Commerce, who favoured the enhancement of existing technical teaching capacity in the city, while Alderman Stringer, the leader of the City Council, was concerned about the financial implications for the city. In spite of the obvious divisions of opinion, a Council for the Establishment of a University was established, the membership including the Lord Mayor, Gorton, Field, Weaver, Richardson, Rees, Roberts and Edgar Letts, the editor of the *Coventry Evening Standard*, with Richardson as secretary. The Council was not a heavyweight body and it was significant that Stringer was not a member. The Lord Mayor did not attend and W. H. Stokes, a former trades unionist who had been Chairman of the Midland Regional Board for Industry, took over the chairmanship; some of its members, notably Field and Weaver, were opponents of the idea from the start.

In the two years of its life – it was disbanded on a 12-6 vote in April 1956 – the Council held only five meetings.[11] The first in May 1954 received a paper unsigned but obviously the work of Gorton entitled 'Aims' which argued for a university closely linked to the technologies of the region but including some humanities, as at MIT and Cal Tech, along with urban planning, the study and solution of social problems, industrial relations, and the study of business and public authority management.[12] Gorton remained a strong supporter but letters to Richardson indicated his growing pessimism as to the Council's future. In June he was optimistic that a new report from the Parliamentary and Scientific Committee might buttress the case but by August he could see no way forward

---

★The University of Warwick made amends when it awarded Sir Frank Whittle an Honorary Degree in 1968.

but to establish a new and more high powered group to include some outstanding local trades union leaders like Stokes, Taylor of the Amalgamated Engineering Union and Jack Jones, the Regional Secretary of the Transport and General Workers Union, together with employer representatives from companies like Rootes, the Standard Motor Company, Jaguar, Armstrong Whitworth, Courtaulds and GEC. Local politicians, local enthusiasts and bishops, he thought, should keep out. His last letter dated 16 May 1955 warmly supported a draft report prepared by Richardson recommending the establishment of an 'Institute of Technology of university standing similar to those of MIT or Cal Tech though on a smaller scale'.[13] His death shortly afterwards was to rob the Council of its major voice. The extent to which the Council had been stalled can be judged by a letter from Richardson to the Lord Mayor, to whom the draft report had been sent for comment some months previously, urging that 'the best memorial to the memory of a good and remarkable man would be to make sure that this part of his work is carried on'.[14] But the internal opposition was too great. The Council's final report, heavily amended from Richardson's first draft, concluded that the creation of a university was impossible at that time, and not likely to be possible in the near future without a change of national policy. It therefore recommended concentrating on the upgrading of technical education in Coventry.[15] Caution and the more educationally conservative arguments had won the day.

In fact the Council was doomed to failure from the start by the position adopted both by the Government and the UGC. The arguments put forward for new institutions in the Tawney/Tizard UGC paper were almost instantly foreclosed by the existing universities' willingness to expand to the number of students that the Barlow Report had called for. In 1952, following the House of Lords debate, the UGC was invited to advise 'how best rapidly to build up at least one institution of university rank devoted predominantly to the teaching and study of the various forms of technology'[16], and it was left open to them to propose a new technological university. But the Committee came down decisively against on the grounds that the length of time which it would take to plan and develop such an institution would mean that it could make no contribution to solving current manpower problems. It was easy to forget, it said, that MIT's reputation was not created overnight but was the result of 'slow growth which cannot be forced'.[17] There was another important argument, which had particular relevance for the university that was ultimately founded in Coventry. Ever since the UGC had considered the inclusion of the university colleges at Nottingham, Reading and Southampton on the grants list in the 1920s it had had an unspoken criterion that university institutions should have at least two faculties so that interchanges between sciences and the arts could be encouraged.[18] In the 1952-3 discussions the Committee recorded that 'we considered it was imperative to keep applied science in the closest possible touch with the pure sciences, and we also attached importance to contact with the humanities, many of whose disciplines are becoming increasingly recognised as a necessary part of the education of technologists'.[19] In January 1953, the UGC announced that it intended to concentrate funds on building up Imperial College (which fulfilled its criteria because it was part of the University of London). Later in the year, when further funds were made available for technological education, they were used to prime developments at existing universities in Glasgow, Manchester, Leeds, Birmingham, Bristol, Cambridge and Sheffield. In the same year the Committee had turned down a renewed application for university status from Bradford unless it sought Faculty status from the University of Leeds (a subservience that the proud citizens of Bradford rejected out of hand).

There was thus never any chance even if the Council had brought forward a positive recommendation that it would have been credible nationally. The UGC records show that no formal approach was made to them, though a letter from Richardson, seeking information about national higher education statistics, is preserved in their files.[20] In Coventry the impact of the 1956 White Paper on Technical Education which had listed Rugby's technical college, and not Coventry's, as one of the country's leading colleges, acted as a spur to establishing a new college (subsequently the Lanchester College) to gain Regional College of Technology status.[21] A subsequent Ministry of Education circular envisaged that some of these colleges might be designated as Colleges of Advanced Technology (CATs).[22] Having been bypassed once Coventry saw this as a more realistic ambition than the much more speculative and less locally focussed claim for a university for which there was apparently no influential or serious political support.

The campaign to secure a university

Gorton's ideas and the work of the Council had never seriously got off the ground because they had failed either to capture the unequivocal support of the Coventry City Council or any other local heavyweight political body, nor had they engaged with the one national agency which was concerned with university planning, the UGC. Where Brighton, York and Norwich had been given clear encouragement by the UGC to return to the attack when economic circumstances and evidence of student demand warranted it, Coventry had failed even to register a formal interest in the idea of bidding for a university. Yet just two months before the Council disbanded itself, W. G. Stone, the Director of Education for Brighton, wrote a memorandum to the UGC setting out the national demographic trends and the increasing staying-on rate in the sixth form as part of an argument for re-opening the case for a University College in Brighton. The UGC itself paid tribute to this memorandum as being one of the formative influences on the policy to create the New Universities.[23]

It is worth asking why Coventry and Warwickshire were not at this time fertile ground for the launching of a university idea. Warwickshire, which was to play a larger part later, is easily accounted for. Very much a county authority, it had developed

Rugby's technical college to nationally recognised status, but in higher education it traditionally looked to Birmingham, and (like Coventry) made an annual financial contribution from the rates to the University there.[24] The relationship between the County Council and the City Council was strained not only by boundary disputes where the County saw Coventry as seeking to expand at its expense but at a political level where the Labour majority in Coventry was seen as giving encouragement to a growing Labour minority in Warwickshire. Personal relationships between Sir Edgar Stephens, Clerk to the County Council for forty years, and the Town Clerks of Coventry, Fred Smith and, after 1946, Charles Barratt, were somewhat less than cordial.

Coventry was much the more dynamic local authority and with its massive programme for the reconstruction of the city centre had a great deal more to be dynamic about. Labour had secured a majority in the municipal elections for the first time in 1937 and was to rule Coventry for an unbroken period of 30 years. The Labour leadership in these years was of outstanding quality – Halliwell, Stringer, Hodgkinson, Callow and Waugh – and their ideas and the imaginative plans for redevelopment after the Blitz attracted an equally able group of chief officers – Smith and Barratt as Town Clerk, Donald Gibson to be succeeded by Arthur Ling as City Architect and Planning Officer, Ford the City Engineer, Sydney Larkin succeeded by Dr A. H. Marshall as City Treasurer, and Walter Chinn as Director of Education. The City Officers were not always easy bedfellows. Many had earned their seniority from within the Corporation and had grown up with the robust view of politics that seems always to have held sway in Coventry. Others like Gibson and Ling came from outside and were determined to retain a degree of independence that fitted somewhat uneasily into any kind of corporate style. What united them, however, was a belief in the re-development of the city and they were led, from 1946, by Charles (later Sir Charles) Barratt, one of the most influential city managers of his generation.[25]

At the political level the Coventry Labour administration derived its authority and style from the powerful Coventry trades unions and co-operative movement and every major decision to be taken in open Council was pre-decided by a Labour group meeting and then discussed in the Policy Advisory Committee which was the central committee for the conduct of business. The Party as a whole and, perhaps particularly Stringer and Hodgkinson who were the dominant personalities of the period in which the University was founded, were genuinely imbued with a determination to achieve a Socialist society and saw the rebuilding of Coventry from the redevelopment of Broadgate to the establishment of a civic theatre and a civic art gallery in this light.[26]

From 1945 to the late 1950s the main energies of the City Council were devoted to the replanning and rebuilding of the city. With its strong attachment to apprenticeship schemes and its close working knowledge of industry it was natural that in education its interests lay in the provision of more and better schools and in technical education. Of the civic leaders only Hodgkinson had personal experience of higher education, through study at Ruskin College, but both he and Stringer had a broad vision of the benefits that university education could bring to the culture of the city. They were also political realists and saw little point in expending energies on lost causes. On the other hand there was probably a grain of truth in the accusation by Letts that the City Council had not given proper support to the university proposal because it 'came from outside their ranks'.[27]

The demise of the Council for the Establishment of a University caused not a ripple in the political life of Coventry. Barratt's diaries and the memories of senior officers still living suggest that it made no impact on the city although the ideas it generated remained in the minds of some of those involved, most notably Henry Rees whose enthusiasm for the project appears to have been undiminished when in every formal sense it was dead and buried. Indeed, at the request of Walter Chinn, almost the final act of the University Promotion Committee at its last meeting in April 1965 was to record Rees' role in being 'largely responsible for keeping the idea of a university alive in the 1950s and for helping to bring it forward at the right time to be taken up by the Government'.[28]

What happened was that a change of heart had taken place at national level about the future direction of universities. In 1954 and 1955 the official view was that student numbers were if anything slowing down and there was a serious danger of having to lower standards to maintain the level of intake. Two demographic factors were to shake this complacency. The first was the effect of the post-war bulge in births which was forecast to produce a peak in the 18-year-old age group between 1964 and 1967 and the second was evidence of an increased staying-on rate in the schools. In 1956 the Treasury was basing its forecasts on 106,000 university students in the mid-1960s but by 1958 it had raised the figure to 124,000, while the Association of University Teachers (AUT) in the same year estimated 145,000. The Treasury's 1958 forecast accompanied a statement of building grants to universities which included a provisional allocation for a new University College of Sussex at Brighton. This announcement was the result both of the Stone memorandum to the UGC, referred to above, and the energy that Brighton Borough Council had put in to reviving its case for a university. Whereas previously it had sought an institution based on Brighton alone, now it had brought in the support of the neighbouring authorities of East and West Sussex and Eastbourne and Hastings (with the name accordingly changing from Brighton to Sussex), and it had offered Stanmer Park as a site. The February announcement in *The Times* alerted Rees to the change of circumstances and he immediately began contacting City officers, notably Chinn and Ling, to energise them into mounting a case for Coventry. On Chinn's advice he secured an interview with the Vice-Chancellor of Birmingham, Sir Robert Aitken. The University of Birmingham's attitude was important in two ways: first, one argument that had been deployed in earlier discussions was that there was no requirement for another university in the West Midlands and that Birmingham could satisfy local needs, and the second was that Birmingham's active sponsorship of a Coventry bid would give it greatly increased academic respectability. At the meeting Aitken gave reassurance and support to a Coventry proposal and indicated his willingness to mention the matter to Sir Keith Murray, the Chairman of the UGC. Birmingham had already started a substantial building programme and accepted that it could not expand faster than these plans allowed.[29] Aitken's support for a new university in Coventry was to go much beyond this as will be evident below.

By June Rees was himself writing to the Chairman of the UGC arguing the case and setting out a list of possible academic departments which he said he had drawn up after consultation with Chinn. The UGC's acknowledgement was bland and rather pointedly said they looked forward to hearing further from Mr Chinn in due course.[30] Unabashed, Rees wrote to Murray again in early October to let him know unofficially the progress being made in Coventry.[31]

In the meantime Rees had recruited another 'irregular' to his cause in the shape of Arthur Ling. Ling was a distinctly untypical City Officer. Following in Gibson's footsteps he had adopted the practice of using the resources of his office to develop planning ideas and models for public consultation before the projects had been given preliminary consideration within the City Council machinery. Moreover he was used to attracting press attention to particular ideas independently of the Corporation or the Town Clerk. This could produce convulsions of bureaucratic or political fury, but he justified it as introducing greater openness and more ideas into what was after all one of the most forward looking planning and redevelopment schemes in Europe. Rees describes in his book how he identified a site on Corporation land bounded by the Kenilworth and Gibbet Hill Roads and Ling confirms that it was Rees who took him out to see it.[32]★ Ling was an ideal collaborator for such a project and in September 1958 he published a model and an imaginative development plan for a University College in Coventry which was given extensive coverage in *The Times*, the *Manchester Guardian* and later in the *Architects Journal*. The Ling plan was quite different from earlier ideas, such as Gorton's. It proposed 'a self-contained community complete in every respect, a place where the pursuit of knowledge and the life of the community would be synonymous'. Thus academic departments (a list of which had been drawn up in consultation with Chinn) 'would be closely linked with the buildings in which the students lived and spent their leisure time'.[33]

As an alternative to the Gibbet Hill location he listed a seven acre city centre site south-east of the cathedral around Whitefriars and Much Park Streets. This was very much a second best included to meet potential City Council criticism and both he and Chinn greatly preferred the out-of-town site. The Ling *démarche* earned him a severe rebuke from Barratt on behalf of the Policy Advisory Committee for 'a patent flouting of their previous instructions'.[34] His response, characteristically unrepentant, argued that the success of the proposal in the public mind 'is due to the combined public

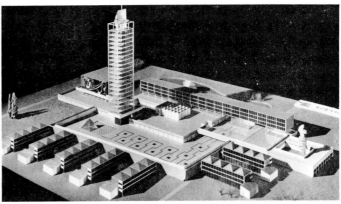

University model, designed by Arthur Ling, showing a 'tower of learning' in the centre of the campus.

and private initiative'[35]. There is no doubt that the appearance of an apparently well worked out architectural plan, on land which had been purchased from the Leigh estate by a far-sighted City Council in the 1920s, created an immediate wave of support for the university idea amongst Stringer, Hodgkinson and other prominent councillors as well as more generally in the city and the county.

Simultaneously Chinn submitted a 'Memorandum on the Creation of a University in Coventry' to the Education Committee. Whereas Ling's ideas about a university were primarily architectural and viewed from a living and communal perspective, Chinn approached it as an extension of his ideas about education in general. A socialist himself and a Quaker, he had a strong admiration for Tawney and the Keele University experiment. His Memorandum conceded that the case for a university was not the education of local students because 'a university is by its very nature non-local in character', and should not be put forward for reasons of local prestige 'but because of the very great practical value to the pattern of communal life which would be added to if the University thread could be woven into it'. Some universities were getting too big, and he regretted that Keele was planning to grow beyond its original target of 600 to 1,200 students. 'Coventry would certainly not wish to go beyond that figure'. Relations would need to be worked out with the City of Coventry Training College, and the plans for the new College of Technology, which would not however conflict with a university and 'might well provide the equivalent of a Faculty of Engineering'.[36]

The idea of new universities had captured the national mood with the foundation of Sussex. But in Coventry it was given a further push by the publication in May of a *Report on a Policy for*

★This site was subsequently significantly altered both because parts of it were unsuitable for building and to provide a better fit with the later gift of land from Warwickshire. The effect was to reduce the allocation of land near the Kenilworth Road (thus leaving the East Site on which buildings were being constructed somewhat isolated) and moving the main site of the University further up Gibbet Hill Road.

University Expansion by the AUT.[37] Nationally this Report was influential in its forecast of student demand but from the Coventry point of view the greatest impact was in its list of proposed sites for new universities which included, somewhat surprisingly, Leamington Spa. How Leamington came to be named is not clear – the Town Clerk of Leamington immediately disclaimed all knowledge of the proposal – but the effect on Coventry was immediate. The Labour group in Coventry were already fully converted to the case for a university but the Conservatives, led by Councillor G. S. N. Richards, had been less convinced, citing the proximity of Birmingham and other universities in Leicester, Nottingham and Oxford and the need not to be distracted from the provision of good technical education. But, as Richards was to say in the Council Chamber, if a university was to be established anywhere in the West Midlands it had to be in Coventry.[38]

The decision of the Policy Advisory Committee to support the proposal, followed by all party support at the meeting of the City Council on 2 December put the planning of the campaign for a university on an altogether different basis. First and foremost, it took it away from the 'irregulars' and put it squarely in the hands of Barratt and Chinn. Secondly, the decision to offer a site for a university, on the basis of the original site proposed by Ling, meant that the city had become an active contributor to the project and had a vested interest in its success. There was also a third factor. Chinn in his initial memorandum had specifically discounted the factor of local prestige but there is no doubt that the leadership of the City Council saw the university project as part of the development of the city and as in line with the establishment of the Belgrade Theatre, the Herbert Art Gallery and the support for the School of Music as a further step in bringing a stronger cultural and intellectual element into the life of what had been primarily a manufacturing city. In another way it balanced the great project to rebuild the cathedral which was even then in the construction stage. In the Coventry of those days the momentum of redevelopment was such that anything seemed possible. As Barratt was to write to an objector to the university bid some eighteen months later: 'it is a chance for the future of the city which should not be missed, otherwise we shall bitterly regret not having made the attempt'.[39]

The marshalling of the campaign to bring a university to Coventry rested firmly in the hands of Barratt and there is no reason to doubt Bishop Bardsley's judgment: 'The enterprise depended to a very large extent on the Town Clerk, without whose enthusiastic, knowledgeable and capable assistance it could hardly have succeeded'.[40] Indeed any reading of the files in the UGC, the Coventry Record Office and the University and of other material not merely confirms this but emphasises the commitment and sheer professionalism which Barratt brought to the task. Less happy when dealing with the Academic Planning Board which he confesses in his diaries to be 'quite an intellectual exercise', a shorthand for saying that he sometimes found difficulty in grasping what direction, if any, the discussion was taking, he was a master of the art of contacting the right people, bringing them together, keeping them

to timetables, balancing points of view, and driving forward when the essential details were in place. And it must be realised that this had to be carried on top of the already immensely heavy duties of managing the reconstruction of Coventry, the considerable routine political and civic demands of his job, which included receiving countless international delegations to view the Coventry redevelopment plan, and a substantial portfolio of external professional commitments. Reflecting nearly a decade later on the events of the period 1959 to 1962 Sir Arnold Hall concluded that he had 'no doubt that the true originator of this University was Charles Barratt in his capacity as Town Clerk . . . very few, except those who worked closely to him on it, probably realise the enormous amount of time, energy and emotion that he put into it at that time and I am quite sure it wouldn't have started without him'.[41] While we may question the word 'originator', that he was the linchpin of the effort over this period to bring the University into existence is beyond doubt.

In December 1958 no decision had been announced to embark on a programme of founding any further universities after Sussex. The AUT Council, however, passed a motion welcoming Coventry's initiative and in January Henry Maddick, a member of Birmingham University's staff and convenor of the AUT's University Development Committee, wrote to Barratt to offer AUT advice and support[42] and it was through the agency of Lord Chorley, the Honorary General Secretary of the AUT, that the first substantive contact was made with the UGC. Indeed a note on the UGC file indicates some alarm at the prospect that Coventry might be receiving advice from the AUT rather than the UGC[43] and a first meeting of Barratt and Chinn with the Chairman of the UGC was accordingly arranged.

Meantime, Barratt was making the first moves to broaden the constituency of support for a university. H. T. Chapman, Managing Director of Armstrong Siddeley (and a distinguished aircraft engine designer), agreed to host a meeting of industrialists over dinner at Barford House to give Barratt and Chinn the opportunity to get their support.[44] The make-up of the meeting is interesting not only because many of those present were to play significant roles in the University subsequently but because of what it tells us about the industrial make-up of Coventry. The most significant figure was undoubtedly Sir Arnold Hall. Chapman knew Hall because they were both directors of the Hawker Siddeley Group and invited him specifically because of his academic background. Hall was an FRS and had been a professor at Imperial College at the age of 30, before moving into industry. Also present were Sir William Lyons (Jaguar), Sir Stanley Harley (Coventry Gauge and Tool), Col. Clarke (Alfred Herbert), J. Wright (Dunlop), W. G. Rootes (Humber, and Lord Rootes' brother), H. Heath (Coventry Radiators), R. E. Robinson (GEC), J. E. Pedder (Courtaulds) and A. W. Weeks (Engineering Employers Association).★ The meeting was not a success. Chapman, Hall, Harley and Rootes supported the proposal with varying degrees of enthusiasm but there were serious criticisms from some of the others: it was premature to talk of a university before the new technical college was established, Coventry was not an ideal place to found a university – Coventry industry was more interested in applied than pure science, Coventry industry would have 'little or no interest in a local university'.

Barratt recorded in his diary that it was 'a depressing experience' and Hall described it as 'a very cool reception altogether'. Hall went on to say that Barratt was 'more upset than I have ever seen him', as well he might have been as he was due to see the UGC in less than a fortnight's time, but Hall comforted him by prophesying that this was not the final word and that industry would come round. Hall's forecast proved to be correct for a second meeting held less than a year later was entirely positive in its support.

The meeting with the UGC was more encouraging. Murray based his remarks on a statement he had made to a delegation from Gloucester and Cheltenham a week or so earlier: there was no decision yet on whether there were to be new universities or if there were, how many; a new university should not be entirely dependent on the UGC and the UGC would therefore expect Coventry and local industry to indicate the level of local interest and how much they would be prepared to contribute; the UGC accepted the idea of a high proportion of students being in residences but in the long term accommodation would be required in the community; the site provided would need to be 200 acres; the university needed to plan for at least 2,000 students to take advantage of economies of scale; a local committee needed to be set up outside the City Council; academic plans should be kept to generalities for the time being.[45] With this crucial information as to what the UGC was looking for, the Policy Advisory Committee decided in September 1959 to invite the Lord Mayor to secure a broadly based University Promotion Committee. In effect this handed over the matter to Barratt.

The identification of a chairman was obviously a crucial first step. (Gloucester and Cheltenham had the Duke of Beaufort.) In his diary Barratt set out his criteria:

> he must be a public figure with political influence which we might wish to use; he must have some local connection without being so local as to arouse jealousies locally; he must at the lowest be not *persona non grata* with the Council – and that could be tricky; ideally he must be able to influence the essential financial support of industry and yet ought to be an acceptable figure in the academic world – and of course he must be persuaded before we had gone very far that the idea was a good one.[46]

Sir Arnold Hall might have seemed an obvious figure but he made it clear from the outset that he would only serve as Vice-Chairman. Barratt then approached Lord Tedder who was both Chancellor of Cambridge and Chairman of Standard Triumph but he declined on grounds of pressure of work. In his book Rees claims to have suggested Lord Rootes' name to Barratt but in his diaries Barratt describes it as the outcome of a conversation with Hall.[47] At any rate Barratt went to see Rootes, whom he knew well, at Devonshire House in Piccadilly on 1 January 1960. Rootes did not accept immediately and said he must think it over and 'would only be willing to take on the job if he thought we had a sporting chance of success'.[48] A fortnight later he agreed. It was a master stroke. Lord 'Billy' Rootes had close links with Coventry. He had served an apprenticeship with Singers Motors Ltd in Coventry before the First World War (and had bought the company 42 years later) and, having established the Rootes dealership chain†, bought the Humber and Hillman car companies in Coventry, his brother W. G. (later Sir Geoffrey) Rootes becoming Chairman and Managing Director. He later took over Sunbeam, Talbot and Karrier to create the Rootes Group which was among the first to join the Government's 'shadow factory' scheme in Coventry for aircraft production. On the day after the Coventry Blitz he was made chairman of the Industrial Reconstruction Committee and in four weeks to the day he could claim that electricity, gas, water and telephones had been restored to all the engineering factories engaged in war production and everyone was back at work. Above all else he was a 'super salesman' constantly called upon by successive Governments during and after the war, perhaps most notably as chairman of the Dollar Exports Council set up in 1951 during the dollar crisis, for whom it is said he flew 70,000 miles at his own expense to sell British business abroad. In an unforgettable tribute to him in his first Report to the Court of the University, Jack Butterworth wrote:

> Once his interest and enthusiasm were aroused not for one moment did his mind sleep and when the searchlight beam of his intellect focussed on a matter for action he tore into it. He was a demon for tackling a problem and a perfectionist in his handling of one; he was a man who got things done and was thorough in everything he did. Billy Rootes was indomitable, exuberant and tireless; absolutely forward looking and, at seventy, so often ahead in vision and energy of most of his younger associates. There was great strength about him, compounded of experience, stubbornness and personal determination. He was a man who took decisions and whose decisions almost invariably proved his judgment right. He did not always ride unchallenged and if his determination to be in the lead sometimes caused resentment people generally fell in behind him and certainly it was not possible for anyone

*Hall was to become the first Pro-Chancellor and Chairman of the University Council, and was succeeded in that position by Harley. Lyons was to become a founder member of Council. Clarke's successor at Alfred Herbert, Sir Richard Young, was to become a long serving member, while Pedder was to introduce his colleague R. J. Kerr Muir into the University discussions and he became the first Honorary Treasurer. Barratt himself was to become a founder member of the Council.

†At his death the Rootes dealers established the Lord Rootes Memorial Fund to encourage students to undertake adventurous projects in the summer vacation.

to remain long at odds with Lord Rootes. The proportion of charm in his make-up was dangerously high and brought many a bird off the bush.[49]★

Perhaps in these first days of the Promotion Committee another characteristic was important: 'If there were strings to pull, arms to twist and people to stir into activity, here was a master of these arts'.[50] As Chairman of the Committee he was a dominant figure. With Barratt as secretary, meetings were always well prepared by pre-meeting discussion, and they were conducted briskly and with little discussion and no dissent. Colleagues recall that Barratt who played a full part in City Council meetings said little at meetings of the Promotion Committee. In his diary Barratt described the Rootes/Hall partnership as 'almost an ideal combination'[51] and in 1964 as the Charter and Statutes were being drawn up with Rootes designated as the first Chancellor and Hall as the first Pro-Chancellor and Chairman of Council he took justifiable pride in his role in persuading them to take on the leadership of the campaign.[52] If Rootes was the figurehead, the publicist and in many ways the driving force, it was Hall who consistently supplied the balance of academic and practical judgment. At many critical moments it was Hall who played the more important role.

While Barratt was putting these key appointments in place a sense of extreme urgency was suddenly injected by the UGC. In March 1959 the UGC had set up a New Universities Sub-Committee whose task was to establish criteria for the founding of new universities and to put the claimants into a 'batting order' if new foundations were to be permitted.[53] The Sub-Committee took evidence from a number of sources. It is not necessary here to describe the conflicting advice that this produced except to highlight the consistent view in favour of the importance of student residential arrangements either by the provision of student residences or by the certainty that adequate lodgings were available in the vicinity. One important contribution, of which the Coventry team were apparently unaware, was a paper by Professor W. G. V. Balchin of University College, Swansea, published in March in the *New Scientist* but sent privately to the UGC.[54] The paper argued that the distribution of the existing universities had come about as a product of population and in response to national, regional or civic needs but

> The national and civic forces which have produced the greater part of the present pattern are now largely satisfied. Only one further city – Coventry – has in recent years grown to the quarter of a million level of population and now aspires to its own university college. Its ambitions are clearly in accord with the general evolving pattern.

The UGC found Balchin's general thesis that the location of universities should be based on population and 'a radius of significant influence' compelling and there is evidence that it influenced both Murray and the New Universities Sub-Committee.[55]

In the last days of December, Murray wrote to Barratt to say that the UGC would be making its recommendations to the Chancellor of the Exchequer in June 1960 and a Coventry bid was required by early April. Murray wrote rather testily in the margin of Barratt's somewhat surprised reply that he could not think what was holding them up and that Coventry had been less active than Norwich or York or even Gloucester and Cheltenham.[56] At the meeting of the New Universities Sub-Committee in late January he commented that Coventry had not yet even appointed the chairman of its Promotion Committee.[57] At that stage Norwich and York had already submitted their bids and their delegations had met the Sub-Committee. Gloucester and Cheltenham's bid was in, Stevenage hoped to submit soon, a delegation was shortly expected from Essex, Kent would be in by June. Some others had fallen by the wayside – Hereford, Bournemouth and Whitby – and nothing had recently been heard from Lancaster.[58] If Coventry was not to miss the bus it had only three months. It was the sort of challenge which Barratt almost enjoyed.

His first move was to persuade the Lord Mayor to bring together an informal group. This comprised Bishop Cuthbert Bardsley, Lord Iliffe (the proprietor of the *Coventry Evening Telegraph*), Lord Tedder, Lord Rootes, the Rev Lincoln Minshall (a survivor with Rees from the Council for the Establishment of a University), Philip Rendall from Courtaulds, Alderman Howard (the Chairman of the County Council), Alderman B. H. Hunt (Chairman of the County Education Committee), Sir Edgar Stephens (Clerk to the County Council), Alderman Stringer as Chairman of the Policy Advisory Committee, Alderman Callow (Chairman of the Coventry Education Committee), Alderman Hodgkinson, Sir Robert Aitken (Vice-Chancellor of Birmingham), Rees, Barratt and Chinn. The list was, he confided to his diary, 'a minor headache to produce'.[59] A prime objective was of course to secure Warwickshire's support. The creation of an independent Promotion Committee was a first step because the County would not have joined a Coventry-led campaign. But as far back as September Barratt and Chinn had been discussing tactics. Rather than approach Stephens who they were sure would raise difficulties, Chinn was delegated to talk to Yorke Lodge, the County Education Officer and, through him, Howard. Howard, however, was concerned that some County Councillors would view support for a University of Coventry, with the implication that it involved a gift of land, as yet another attempt by the City to expand its boundaries at Warwickshire's expense. Chinn therefore suggested changing the name of the university to the University of Mid Warwickshire[60] and it was this concession that enabled Howard to join the informal group.

A meeting of the group was planned for 8 March but a pre-meeting over lunch was held on 4 March and at the request of the County representatives discussion centred on the name of the university.[61] Chinn floated the title already proposed to Howard

---

★This last sentence refers to his powers as a fund raiser which is described in more detail in the Appendix on the Foundation Fund Appeal.

but Bishop Bardsley immediately jumped in to argue that it was cumbersome and seemed to have a ring of mediocrity about it. He then proposed 'the University of Warwick'. Hodgkinson responded that Coventry did not care what its name was as long as the bid was successful and the meeting immediately agreed it. At this point, however, the County Council representatives tried to argue that they would be unable to commit themselves to a Promotion Committee without formally seeking a mandate from their Council but Aitken turned on them so vigorously that they agreed to proceed. At the formal meeting four days later Rootes was confirmed as chairman, Hall vice-chairman, the name was adopted, an informal assurance was given by Rootes that he could raise £1m for student residences, the City representatives reported they would offer the University recurrently the proceeds of 1d rate, and the County representatives were commissioned to secure the support of the district authorities in Warwickshire. On 15 March Howard was able to tell Barratt that he had cleared his lines with his members and invitations were sent out to 270 industrialists and local dignitaries to attend a first meeting of the Promotion Committee on 28 March.

Hall, who had to chair the meeting in Rootes' absence in the USA, said later that he 'had the greatest qualms . . . about this because I thought that maybe only half a dozen people would turn up'.[62] He need not have worried. It was according to the *Coventry Evening Standard* 'a packed chamber in the Council House': even at such short notice 130 attended.[63] The meeting confirmed all the decisions of the Lord Mayor's informal group, with Howard paying tribute to Coventry's concession over the name of the University, and a unanimous vote supported the creation of the University. Summing up the case Hall said, 'A University in Coventry would reflect local interests but we are going forward with a general case on a broad front'.[64] After the vote a message was read out from Lord Iliffe pledging the first £10,000 of an appeal. Two days later the 'Case for the Establishment of a University of Warwick' was dispatched to the UGC. The document had substantially been drafted by Chinn in consultation with Rees but the orchestration of events was the work of Barratt. 'A most satisfying bit of backroom work', he commented in his diary.[65]

But it was not all sweetness and light. Although many of those who could not attend the meeting wrote letters of support, the view was not unanimous. One replied, for example, 'that another university [in the region] would be extravagant, unnecessary and ill conceived' and that 'it would be better to spend further money on the provision of technical education at a lower level'.[66] The change of name too brought some criticism. Richardson wrote to suggest 'the University of Arden'.[67] Letts wrote to protest that the name should remain the University of Coventry.[68] It is perhaps fortunate that the County was unaware that at least in Barratt's mind the thought remained that the name might revert back if the bid was successful, because the County, reluctant at first, were to commit themselves wholly to the project, with material contributions on the same scale as Coventry's – a gift of £92,000 to enable the

University to acquire a further 200 acres of Warwickshire land on the other side of Gibbet Hill Road, and the proceeds of 1d rate.★ The subsequent success of the Foundation Fund Appeal amongst Warwickshire residents (see Appendix page 124) is a testimony to the County's enthusiasm for the university idea. Barratt's later statement that the history of the University would 'stand as a shining example of generous and whole hearted collaboration' between the two authorities was perhaps overstated if applied to the whole course of this history but certainly was true once the two authorities had committed themselves.[69]

The UGC's reaction to 'The Case' was entirely favourable. Syers, the Secretary of the UGC, in a note to Murray called it 'a workmanlike document' which answered most of the points on which information was needed.[70] The visit of the Coventry delegation, however, seemed inauspicious. First, neither Rootes nor Hall could be available so that Barratt himself had to be the

The University Promotion Committee visits the UGC, 1960.

spokesman for the delegation. Second, in April the UGC had announced that the Norwich and York bids had been successful and on the day of the meeting with the UGC *The Times* carried a statement: 'Coventry is only one of many towns that have entered for the new university stakes and it is not a heavily backed runner'.[71] The University delegation need not have been concerned. The UGC files suggest that Coventry always had a strong case provided it could get its act together. The City was after all the nearest thing to a 'new university' itself amongst British cities. The support for the University that had been put together was, in the end, broadly based and included a powerful industrial lobby. It had on offer an excellent site. Moreover, what the Coventry delegation

---

★The gift, however, did not take place until 1963 and was negotiated by the Vice-Chancellor after his arrival. The case submitted to the UGC was based on the Coventry land.

did not know was that the Gloucester and Cheltenham meeting with the UGC had not gone well and that Stevenage's bid had never materialised. There was never a fixed number of new universities that could be founded; the competition was much more against the clock, and whether a case was ready for submission to the Treasury by a certain date. Thanks to Barratt, Coventry met the deadline.

The questioning by the Sub-Committee was of the most factual kind: what was the profile of local industry, were there good schools in the area, what was the state of housing for staff, what was the availability of lodgings? It was this last point that produced the only *frisson* in the delegation because when the intention to raise £1m for student residences was announced Murray said that this could cause embarrassment if new universities, where a supply of lodgings existed, 'were to run too far ahead of the older institutions in this respect'.[72] The delegation managed not to rise to this bait but Barratt commented in his diary 'so what!'.[73] As if to prove they meant business the UGC asked for further memoranda on a number of issues, the most tedious of which was lodgings that even necessitated a visit by a UGC officer later in the year to inspect some hostels that Barratt had unwisely offered as a partial solution. But the basic judgment of the Sub-Committee was that: 'Coventry had merit as a site for a possible university. The City had historic roots and had since the war a new pride and dynamism. The Promotion Committee would need a good deal of help on the academic side'.[74] In July the Sub-Committee visited the site and by January 1961 the Secretary of the UGC (whose timetable had obviously slipped from June 1960) was advising the Treasury that the UGC was likely to be recommending Kent, Essex and Warwick as the three bidders that satisfied their criteria.[75] The dialogue about lodgings was not yet completed but this was only bureaucratic sparring, and on 18 May the Chancellor of the Exchequer announced a favourable decision on the three universities. Lancaster had still to be decided and was not announced until November.

What kind of University?

The hectic period between January and March 1960 when Barratt was marshalling the case for the University, and the subsequent dialogue with the UGC, obscured the fundamental question of what kind of university the various proponents of the idea were seeking. If there could be said to be a majority view in the Council for the Establishment of a University it was for a technological university, reflecting Coventry's industrial and social interests. As we have seen, the UGC's views at that time and subsequently were opposed to this concept and all the evidence to the New Universities Sub-Committee confirmed their belief that universities should not be narrowly specialist or vocational. The Federation of British Industry wanted 'balanced men', a different product from the new CATs which simply 'turned out men with the necessary technical knowledge'.[76] The pervasive attitude to technology was more clearly expressed by the Incorporated Association of Head-

masters who also wanted broadly based institutions and saw the CATs as for students 'who are just below the minimum intellectual standard at present enforced' by entry standards to university.[77] Such views would have been rejected out of hand in Coventry. Chinn, who was a progressive in educational matters and had strongly supported comprehensive schools in Coventry, wanted to see a university that was comprehensive, which covered a wider spectrum of levels than the traditional university model, which was local and vocational in orientation and which would have 'a genuine and realistic relationship to its twentieth century parentage'.[78] While he wanted a broadly based institution which had a national catchment, the Coventry vision was one which integrated the Training College and the Lanchester College of Technology with the new University.

It was perhaps a flavour of this which prompted the UGC's comment about the committee 'needing help on the academic side'. The UGC created a situation of potential tension. On the one hand they 'attached great weight to the local interest and enthusiasm shown by the sponsors' but on the other hand they were very clear that the academic programme was something that the sponsors should not be concerned with.[79] Partly this reflected the need for national planning – at various times medicine, agriculture and architecture were all subjects favoured in Coventry but national needs were already provided for in the university system as a whole. But more important, it arose out of the tradition that universities should only become autonomous after a period of academic supervision. Thus the University Colleges of Reading, Leicester, Hull, Nottingham and the South West (Exeter) grew up under the tutelage of the University of London. Keele was initially sponsored as the University College of North Staffordshire by Oxford, Birmingham and Manchester before achieving full university status. The initial concept of Sussex was as a University College. But the UGC recognised there was now a need for new foundations to move more quickly than in the past to full autonomy, and invented the device of an Academic Planning Board, appointed by the Committee after consultation with the local sponsors, which could act as an academic and constitutional sponsoring body and which could provide the authority for the New Universities to award their own degrees from the outset. Another element, not overtly stated, was that the UGC was also anxious to protect the new foundations from being subject to over-dominant local sponsors, perhaps remembering the case of Nottingham where the UGC had resisted full university status until 1948 because the College was unwilling to amend its statutes to reduce the level of lay control. Amongst the New Universities it seems that it was only at Warwick where such tension might have arisen but this was not because of a wish to exercise control so much as because the local sponsors had alternative views as to how they thought the University should develop.

The UGC moved fairly quickly to establish an Academic Planning Board for Warwick comprising Mr E. T. Williams, Warden of Rhodes House, Oxford as its Chairman, Dr (later Sir

James) Cook, Vice-Chancellor of Exeter, Professor L. C. Sykes, Leicester, Professor R. C. Tress, Bristol, Professor R. A. Raphael, Glasgow, Miss E. A. O. Whiteman, Lady Margaret Hall, Oxford, Mr S. F. Burman, Pro-Chancellor of Birmingham, Sir Alan Wilson, Courtaulds (a long-time supporter of a University in Coventry) and Sir Arnold Hall (who had to resign his membership of the Promotion Committee to join the Board). The Board's terms of reference were to establish the academic range of subjects and the general character of undergraduate courses, to prepare draft Charter and Statutes, and to select a Vice-Chancellor, in consultation with the local sponsors, and with him to appoint the first professors.[80] This effectively transferred 'ownership' of the University out of the hands of the Promotion Committee leaving it with primarily a fundraising role. Even though Barratt became the Board's secretary and Hall was a member this caused resentment among many of those who had been most deeply involved in the campaign, especially in Coventry with its strong tradition of managing its own affairs. Those members not engaged in fundraising inevitably felt excluded from the next stages of the action.

There was by no means unanimity locally about what kind of university the sponsors wanted. The Promotion Committee had established an Executive Committee containing most of the members of the original Lord Mayor's informal group, but with some additions, most notably the Director of the Lanchester College, the Principal of Rugby Technical College, the Principal of the Coventry Training College and the headmasters of Rugby School and of King Henry VIII in Coventry. Stimulated by Chinn, a series of informal meetings were held to consider 'the academic content of the University and its contribution to the overall pattern of university education throughout the country' to form the basis of a submission to the Board.[81] Initially these were only meetings of local educationalists but they broadened out and were given formal status as a sub-group of the Executive Committee. Wide consultation with industry and commerce took place in addition to the major educational and research establishments in the area, and a formal Executive Committee submission was made to the Board. The exercise has no parallel in the foundation of the other New Universities.[82]

The Executive Committee of the Promotion Committee, 1961.

There were three broad themes in these discussions: the range of subjects, the academic structure and the relationships with the Colleges. On the first, the group rehearsed again the arguments about whether this was to be a university whose orientation was primarily towards the dominant forces in the local economy or whether it was to be much more broadly based. Kerr Muir from Courtaulds, for example, argued for a 75:25 division of science and arts, Richmond (later Sir Alan), the Director of the Lanchester College, for a technical university of which Lanchester would be the nucleus. Lord Rootes wrote a letter which while accepting that arts must be included argued that 'emphasis should nevertheless be upon automotive, electronic and other engineering aspects as well as commercial studies and modern languages (not dead!)'.[83] Others spoke up vigorously for developing strengths in production engineering. Joan Browne, the Principal of the Training College, and Bishop Bardsley argued for the strong recognition of the humanities and the arts. The argument was only resolved when Hall, who had not at this point moved on to the Academic Planning Board, threw his weight decisively behind a balanced arts and science university and the final proposal was for a division between natural sciences (comprising physics, chemistry, mathematics and some form of biological sciences) and humanities (comprising English, foreign languages, ancient and modern, history, philosophy, political science, the social sciences, economics and geography), with engineering science as a slightly uncertain third area. The second argument revolved around structure. Chinn and Rees were advocates of a non-departmental university based like Sussex and East Anglia (Norwich) on inter-disciplinary schools of studies led by Deans. Dr Templeman, the Registrar of Birmingham, who had come on to the Executive Committee in place of Aitken as Birmingham's representative urged a Part I and Part II system along the lines of the Cambridge Tripos which would provide opportunities for students to change their programme of study after five terms. These two sets of ideas were brought together in the Memorandum to the Board.

The third area, the relationship with Lanchester and the Training College, was complicated by a number of factors, which illustrate only too clearly the difficulty of trying to marry local interests and national policies in higher education. Having come late onto the scene of creating a Regional College of Technology, Coventry did not want to miss the chance of getting it upgraded to a CAT. If Coventry acquired a university would this subsume a CAT, prevent one from being established, or positively assist the case? To make matters worse Coventry could only talk to the Ministry of Education about the future of Lanchester and to the UGC about the University because the UGC was still until 1964 under the Treasury. The UGC was making discouraging noises about starting engineering in any of the New Universities because of the heavy investment in technological education already embarked upon in the mid-1950s. At one point, in order to pacify Lanchester's Director, Templeman proposed that engineering should not be included at all at the University.

The Lanchester problem came to a head when the Lanchester governors decided to launch an appeal for funds to industry to build residences at the college. Such an appeal was bound to compete with the University and in particular with Lord Rootes' commitment to raise a first £1m for residences. After much discussion between the Executive Committee and the Lanchester governors the uncertainty of the future relationship between the two institutions was such that the Lanchester appeal went ahead. This issue highlighted only too publicly the inherent question of the extent to which having two institutions of higher education which seemed in part to duplicate one another could best be solved by full integration or total separation. This theme was to represent a long running and important element in local relationships and in discussions with the Academic Planning Board. The question of the relationship with the Teacher Training College was less contentious but also raised organisational and academic issues.

The Board approached its task from an entirely different standpoint from the Executive Committee.[84] Its members had close personal links with the UGC and with the planning boards of other New Universities and their perspective was national not local. They had a strong Oxbridge orientation (though they showed no interest in following York into a collegiate system) and were determined to make no compromises in guaranteeing the academic excellence of the institution. They were anxious not to ape Sussex and East Anglia by prescribing inter-disciplinarity; they were not much attracted by schools of studies and they were quite opposed to deans. A key element of their approach was that they saw the university growing 'not by seeking to impose upon it at birth an artificial and romantic image of newness but by the choice of staff with ideas on the development of their subjects; and by giving this limited staff the opportunity to create a university and its community'.[85] Finally, they did not wish to commit a vice-chancellor to a plan which he had not had a hand in shaping. When presented with the Executive Committee's memorandum they did not like the idea of trying to marry a Part I and Part II system with schools of studies. They wanted single subject degrees in mathematics, physics, chemistry and engineering science (but thought that biological sciences would have to be deferred, perhaps on advice from the UGC) and, in humanities and social studies, they wanted to see broad first years which led to greater depth in core subjects in the third. Even worse, from the local point of view, they wanted to start on the basis not of those subjects which were advocated locally but those where there was likely to be a strong national demand for students, in which able staff were known to be available and for which there was a career market.

It is easy to see that the two sides were a long way apart and their first joint meeting held in May 1962 was a disaster compounded of mutual incomprehension. On the Executive Committee there was a feeling of 'bitter disappointment' that the proposals were not in their eyes more forward looking[86], on the Board's that they had been criticised unfairly and over-aggressively. Once again Hall emerges in correspondence as playing a key role, defending what he called 'the Coventry atmosphere', commending to the Board that it should 'stick to the path of seeking what is sound and what is good rather than what is different' but also suggesting that the Board 'might itself give thought to the fact that what is different is not necessarily wrong'.[87] Behind the criticisms of the academic programme, however, lay a deep sense of impatience amongst some members of the Executive Committee over the Board's lack of progress in appointing a vice-chancellor. There is no doubt that on many issues Williams simply stalled so as not to commit a new vice-chancellor to a programme on which he had not been consulted. The Board was by no means inactive in its search for the right candidate but it was in competition with many other universities, both new and old. The appointment of Jack (now Lord) Butterworth (Warwick pipping Lancaster at the post for him) gave a new sense of purpose to the whole enterprise and many of the difficulties with the Executive Committee evaporated. A second joint meeting was held and the final submission to the UGC was drawn up harmoniously. Schools of Studies were to be created but around core subjects which would require some concentration from the outset; chairs in mathematics, chemistry, physics, engineering science, economics, philosophy, politics, history, English literature and modern European languages were to be established immediately; and a graduate business school was to be developed. This last idea marked the new Vice-Chancellor's first major impact on the academic planning process and its inclusion in the plan to be submitted to the UGC was as a result of a paper he wrote for the second joint meeting. Lord Rootes had been one of the sponsors of the Franks' review of business education in Britain which had been launched at a dinner at the Rootes headquarters at Devonshire House. But Franks recommended in his Report that the two new business schools he proposed should be at London and Manchester and had ignored the claims of Warwick, to Rootes' considerable chagrin.[88] The Vice-Chancellor's paper had therefore to assume that the business school would be a self-financing venture at least initially. Essentially, in its Report to the UGC, the Board stuck to its basic philosophy. It did not wish to be prescriptive and it wanted to leave the new Vice-Chancellor and his first professorial colleagues the maximum freedom possible to develop the University on their own individual lines.

> We would wish to plan for a beginning with a limited number of Schools which can be done well and from which others will grow. The Vice-Chancellor and the nucleus of the academic staff will wish to map out future academic developments. It is they who will furnish the shape and tone of the new University, they who will patent its eventual stamp.[89]

This philosophy was to serve the University well. The Board found someone in Jack Butterworth who was entirely in sympathy with this approach. There can be no doubt that it has powerfully influenced the University's development.

Lord Rootes launching the University Appeal.

Relations with the Colleges

The Board's report to the UGC left open the question of the relationships with the Training College and the Lanchester and Rugby Colleges. The UGC's reply made it clear that the future of engineering at Warwick 'is undoubtedly affected by the existence of Lanchester College and its potential development'.[90] In the period before the appointment of a Vice-Chancellor Williams had been careful not to enter into any commitments over Lanchester. When a Vice-Chancellor arrived, other priorities immediately took over. Jack Butterworth went into action only two days after his appointment in November 1962. He was faced with a timetable of taking a first student intake in October 1965 with as yet no buildings, no development plan, no architect appointed, and no academic or administrative staff. The question of future relationships with the Lanchester College was necessarily put aside, and was not to be taken up again until 1964. Meantime, the Lanchester governors, supported strongly by Chinn, pressed on with the campaign to secure CAT if not university status; at a meeting with the Department of Education and Science★ in March Chinn believed that he 'received every encouragement immediately to enable (the College) to achieve full university status'[91] though this is contradicted by T. R. Weaver, the civil servant in charge at the DES, who in a note to the UGC said that it was made clear that the Government was not going to declare any more CATs and that Coventry should concentrate on Regional College status.[92] (To set this in context it needs to be recalled that the Robbins Committee, which reported in October 1963, had recommended that the CATs be upgraded to be technological universities. This set aside all the previous UGC objections to giving university status to institutions that were technological only.)

The fall-out from this meeting brought the question of relations between the University and the Lanchester College into immediate focus to the extent that it became in the end an issue of national policy. By 1963-4 the College had over 400 students on advanced full-time courses (rising to 860 in 1964-5) and over 1,000 on part-time non-advanced courses.[93] The future of the College's non-advanced work raised important issues for all parties: for the DES because it believed that Coventry would use them as an argument to seek funding for a new technical college if they were to be jettisoned in a merger; for the UGC because they were courses of sub-degree standard and therefore intrinsically unsuitable to be taught within a university, and for the University because the qualifications and interests of the associated teaching staff did not fit with the research orientation of the staff the University was recruiting. But behind these issues lay the important question of Government policy towards the university and non-university sectors of higher education in the post-Robbins era. A further meeting between Chinn and officials at the Department in late May raised a series of questions about how a take-over could be financed and whether the University was prepared to become 'comprehensive', a matter which they said would need consideration by the UGC. It is clear that the officials were concerned about the precedent which the Coventry situation might create for Brighton where similar discussions were taking place at local level.[94]

On 29 May 1964 the Governors of the College approved in principle a proposal to integrate with the University and in June they asked the University to assume responsibility for the majority of the part-time courses and all the staff. The University was still in its very early stages and only a few staff were on the ground though the professors-elect had been meeting for some time. The University's chief concern lay in the question of how the non-advanced work and the associated staff could fit into the University and the danger that integration would unbalance the University at such an early point in its history. Nevertheless it was already becoming clear that the generous funding implied when the New Universities were founded was beginning to dry up and it looked as if growth was going to be much slower than had been originally forecast. The crucial paper to the Executive Committee of the Promotion Committee was drafted by Hall after a considerable round of local consultation. This suggested that the College should be fully integrated into the University on the basis of a structure which divided it into two departments, a Department of Technology which would include all the full-time degree work and a Department of Extra Mural (Technological) Studies covering the part-time and non-degree-equivalent work which would be headed by Dr Richmond, the then Director. The staff would be divided between the two departments, those in the latter keeping their existing terms of service. On 15 February 1965 this solution was agreed by a historic joint meeting, chaired by Hall, of the Governors of the College, the Executive Committee, the Academic Planning Board and the University, represented by the Vice-Chancellor and the professors-elect.

No doubt such an arrangement would have had its subsequent strains and stresses but it represented a remarkable reconciliation between two different visions of university development, and it offered a genuinely innovative model. Two informal discussions

---

★The Ministry of Education became the Department of Education and Science in 1964 with the transfer of the UGC from the Treasury, and the Science Vote from the Lord President of the Council.

between Chinn and Sir Edward Boyle, the responsible Minister, in June 1964 suggested that there might be trouble ahead. In the first interview Boyle indicated that a binary policy was already being considered and that he was too tidy a planner to envisage disturbance of a well planned development, and in the second, when Sir John Wolfenden, who had succeeded Murray as Chairman of the UGC, also took part, they indicated that it would set a 'dangerous precedent' for other regional colleges and would create a 'second class university'.[95] Soon after this the General Election intervened and with a Labour Government in power it seemed that the proposal might be accepted. Certainly there is evidence that had Richard Crossman, who had been a front bench spokesman on education in opposition, become Secretary of State this might have come about, but he was given Housing instead. On 27 April Anthony Crossland delivered his Woolwich Speech which confirmed the 'dual system' or as it has become known, the 'binary line', between universities and the non-university sector of higher education. None of the reasons for this policy given in his speech justified the rejection of the Lanchester/University case.[96] The true reason, as he spelt it out to a Coventry delegation later in the year, was his determination 'that the maintained system should not be constantly weakened by the loss of its best colleges'.[97] The local bitterness was intense. As Hall was later to say, a remarkable local plan was rejected 'almost without debate since it appeared to violate the principles on which they were considering the evolution of higher education'.[98]

It is perhaps worth quoting Councillor Locksley's statement to the Secretary of State as an epitaph on Coventry's case:

> 'His Authority believed that the whole of education should form a unitary system under State control. They opposed the binary policy principally on the grounds that it would perpetuate what they regarded as artificial divisions between the maintained and the so-called autonomous sector. Advances in the school system had grown out of local experiments. His Authority believed that similar experiments should be allowed in a unitary and comprehensive system of higher education. Coventry appreciated that there were outside pressures being exerted to contain Lanchester within the Government's binary system. However, they believed that an experiment in Coventry would not weaken the Government's hand elsewhere as the situation in Coventry was, in their opinion, already unique. The integration proposals . . . were the natural development of Coventry's desire for a technologically based system of higher education which had been their objective for the last five years' and was supported by local industry.[99]

For Locksley, who had written a supportive letter to the *Coventry Evening Standard* in response to its editorial 'Why not a University for Coventry?' in December 1953, the wheel had come full circle. The result, as we know, was that the Lanchester College became the Lanchester, now Coventry, Polytechnic. For the University, a special UGC/University Study Group on the future of technological education in the region was set up chaired by Dr (now Sir Arthur) Vick★, who had been a member of the UGC's New Universities Sub-Committee. The Study Group recommended that Warwick's engineering should grow to 600 students by the time the University reached 3,000. Because of successive Governments' funding policies, this target was only reached in 1986 when the University total was already 6,000.[100]

In one respect only was the University able to realise the concept of integration with the existing Colleges, and this was with the Training College. Impossible to pursue in 1963-4 because of the Government's rejection of the Robbins recommendation that teacher training colleges should be assimilated into the universities, the opportunity re-emerged with the rationalisation of the colleges of education in the mid-1970s, and in 1978 the Coventry College of Education became the Faculty of Educational Studies in the University. Chinn, from retirement, wrote a warm letter of support to the *Coventry Evening Telegraph* as the negotiations began.

National policy and local aspiration

The history of the establishment of the University is quite unlike that of any other of the New Universities. It was the only New University to be founded in a manufacturing centre and perhaps for this reason the community – at the political, industrial and educational levels – was more involved, and invested more intellectual and, ultimately, financial capital in the university idea than in any of the other New Universities. In these circumstances the difference of approach between the local sponsors and the Academic Planning Board as to what kind of university should be established was perhaps inevitable but both sides were sufficient realists to reach an eventual accommodation, much assisted by the arrival of a Vice-Chancellor who very quickly established close working relationships with the community. In retrospect it can be seen that this tension between local aspiration and national policy created a more interesting environment for a university than one where the local community had no strong views as to the sort of a university it wanted. In a very real sense the University was brought into existence by the generous support of the local authorities and a leading group of industrialists. It could not have happened without the initial leadership of Coventry but it was the very broadly based support of the community as a whole, as evidenced in the success of the Foundation Appeal†, which realised a national policy for founding new universities in the creation of what has become a national institution.

★Sir Arthur Vick was to become Pro-Chancellor and Chairman of Council of the University in 1977.
†For an account of the Foundation Appeal and a full list of contributors see the Appendix, page 124.

A Pictorial Account of the Development of the University

More than any of the New Universities, Warwick's physical aspect illustrates the subordination of the discipline of planning to academic and social demands. The University has had three Development Plans (pages 26 and 27) and has burst out of each of them. The final plan shows the University campus in 1990. The development of the campus is described in three phases. The first (pages 28 to 32) may be ascribed broadly to the 1960s and is associated with the architects Yorke Rosenberg Mardall. The second (pages 33 to 36) covers the 1970s and represents the filling in of the central campus associated mainly with Shepheard and Epstein and Renton Howard Wood. The third phase (pages 37 to 39) shows the effect of the massive building programme of the 1980s, largely funded from non-UGC or UFC sources, and the maturing and greening of the campus. Separate sections are devoted to Gibbet Hill and Westwood (pages 40 and 41).

Notes to the pictures will be found on page 117.

DEVELOPMENT

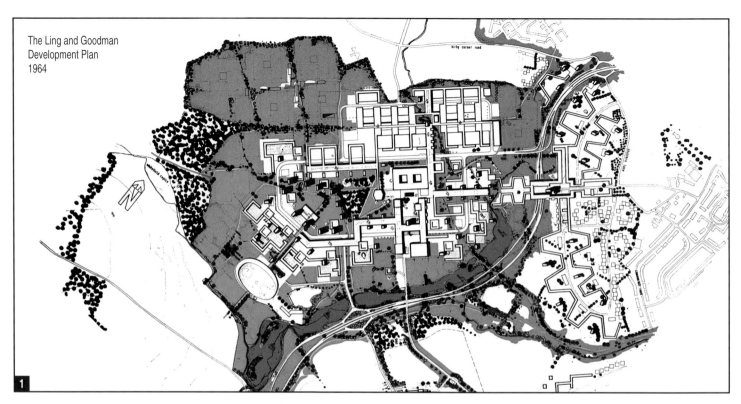

The Ling and Goodman
Development Plan
1964

1

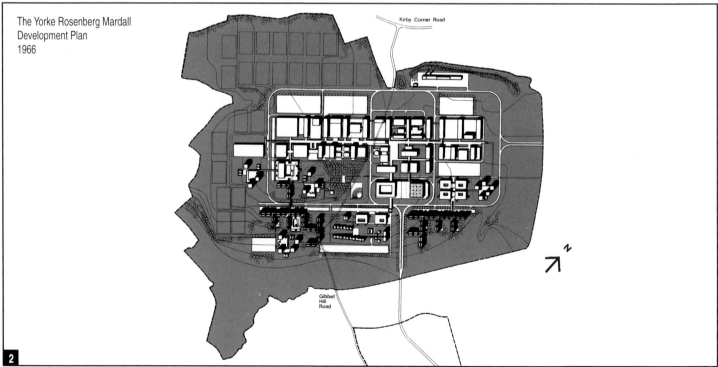

The Yorke Rosenberg Mardall
Development Plan
1966

Kirby Corner Road

Gibbet
Hill
Road

2

The Shepheard and Epstein
Development Plan,
1972

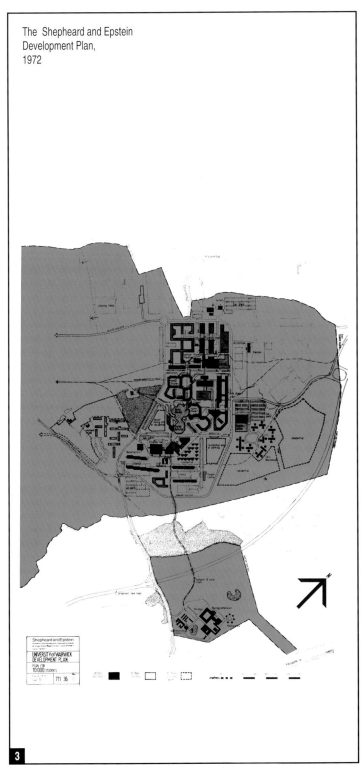

The University Campus,
1990

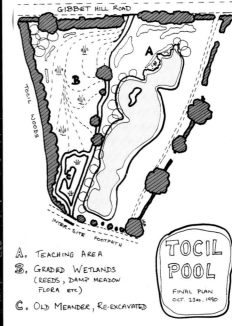

A. TEACHING AREA

B. GRADED WETLANDS
(REEDS, DAMP MEADOW
FLORA ETC)

C. OLD MEANDER, RE-EXCAVATED

TOCIL POOL
FINAL PLAN
OCT. 23RD, 1990

THIRD PHASE

1

2

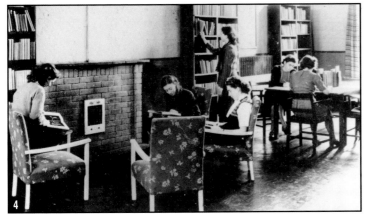

U niversities are made by people – by scholars, by students, by administrators and by staff generally. Warwick's development, more than most universities, has been determined by positive initiatives, by its first Vice-Chancellor, Jack Butterworth, by its first professors and their successors, by generations of lively and critical students, by energetic administrators and by the interaction of personalities and the ideas they generated. The University's atmosphere has encouraged people to be active: there are 250 student clubs and societies; a very significant number of young academic staff have built international reputations in their time at Warwick; subject strengths have grown rapidly round particular individuals and staff they have attracted. This section is divided chronologically between the Sixties, the Seventies and the Eighties, periods that roughly fit changes in the staff and in political and social attitudes on the campus.

Notes to the pictures will be found on page 118.

1 and 2   Jack Butterworth welcomes the first intake

3   The founding Professors

4   The first student Newspaper – *Giblet* – in the making

5, 6, 7   Gay Clifford, David Hutchinson, Hugh Clegg

4 and 5   The first degree ceremony, 1968. Yehudi Menuhin about to receive an honorary degree.
The Chancellor, Lord Radcliffe, leading the academic procession.

6   Rootes resident, 1969

7   Engineering workshops in use

1 Visit by H.M. Queen, 1970

2 The Development Plan Working Party views the Arts Centre site

3 Signing the Students Union building agreement

4 Secretarial staff move into the Senate House

5 An unusual new student, Jack Gowon

6 Greeting the Secretary of State

7 Radio Warwick

A NEW VICE CHANCELLOR

STUDENTS IN THE EIGHTIES

THE PRO CHANCELLOR

STAFF IN THE EIGHTIES

The fundamental task of a University is academic work: teaching, learning and research. Jack Butterworth used to say in his address to new students that the distinguishing feature of University teaching, particularly at Warwick where research flourished, was that it should take students 'to the edge of knowledge in their discipline'. As these pictures try to show, teaching encompasses lecturing, laboratory classes, small group work, seminars, tutorials and projects. It may vary according to discipline and year; it may include off-campus reading weekends, day visits to places which relate to a course, or a term in Venice; above all it is informal, critical and intellectually testing. Warwick's research standing has grown steadily through the 1980s as its academic departments have matured and built international reputations and as externally funded research centres and institutes have proliferated around the campus. In parallel there has been a large expansion in postgraduate study. The University's recognition in the UGC and UFC ratings is charted on page 74 and amongst European Universities in the Carl Bertelsmann Prize 1990 awarded for 'outstanding innovatory ideas and promising initiatives'. But academic study remains an individual, not to say solitary, endeavour as the picture of a student, below, illustrates.

Notes to the pictures will be found on page 119.

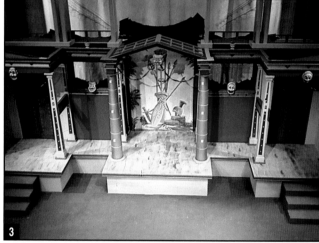

TEACHER TRAINING

1 Field trip

2 Secondary teaching practice

3 Primary teaching practice

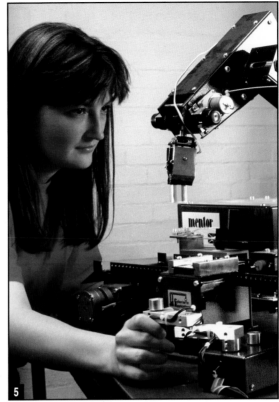

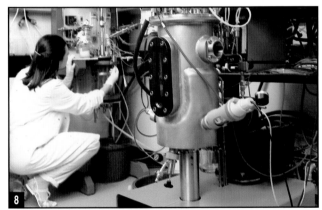

Research in the Biological Sciences

1 — The 1981 cuts

Rank (vertical axis 2–48) vs % Change relative to uniform cut (horizontal axis −40 to +40)

Legend: ● ARTS   ✳ SCIENCE

(chart plotting universities including Brunel, Warwick, UMIST, Essex, East Anglia, York, Bath, St Davids, W Nat Med School, Birmingham, Dundee, Southampton, Kent, Sheffield, Edinburgh, UMIST, Cambridge, Swansea, Oxford, Birmingham, Manchester, Loughborough, London, Leicester, Sussex, Liverpool, Durham, Lancaster, St Andrews, Bath, UWIST, Exeter, Bristol, Durham, Aberdeen, Hull, York, Leeds, Leeds, Edinburgh, Strathclyde, Keele, Liverpool, Southampton, Sheffield, Glasgow, Warwick, City, Glasgow, Manchester, Stirling, Aberdeen, Cardiff, Cambridge, Lancaster, Reading, Reading, Sussex, Exeter, Strathclyde, Newcastle, Oxford, Loughborough, Newcastle, Aberystwyth, Bristol, Dundee, Aberystwyth, Nottingham, Nottingham, Swansea, Cardiff, Leicester, Brunel, Essex, Heriot Watt, Kent, Bangor, Bangor, London, Bradford, Surrey, City, St Andrews, Hull, UWIST, Keele, East Anglia, Aston, Bradford, Surrey, Aston, Heriot Watt, Salford, Salford, Stirling)

WHAT THEY WILL GET

University	86/87 (£m)	% chg 85/86	University	86/87 (£m)	% chg 85/86
Aston	14.939	-0.3	Sheffield	31.507	+0.4
Bath	13.437	+3.6	Southampton	25.465	+3.1
Birmingham	37.622	+0.8	Surrey	12.890	+0.7
Bradford	14.742	+0.7	Sussex	14.349	+2.6
Bristol	29.410	+2.7	Warwick	18.344	+4.0
Brunel	13.014	+0.5	York	11.525	+3.1
Cambridge	43.344	+0.7	**Total England**	**949.333**	**+3.1**
City	11.547	-0.5			
Durham	17.315	-0.5	Aberystwyth UC	10.075	-0.4
East Anglia	14.782	-0.5	Bangor UC	10.906	-0.5
Essex	8.648	+1.4	Cardiff UC	16.965	-0.3
Exeter	15.512	+1.9	St David's, Lamp	1.954	+0.8
Hull	14.278	-0.3	Swansea UC	13.465	-0.5
Keele	8.428	-0.5	UWCM	6.693	+2.7
Kent	10.770	+2.5	UWIST	8.562	+1.5
Lancaster	13.693	+0.7	Welsh Registry	2.202	+1.0
Leeds	42.550	+0.6	**Total Wales**	**70.822**	**+0.2**
Leicester	18.063	+1.7			
Liverpool	37.394	+0.4	Aberdeen	22.035	-0.5
London Bus Sch	1.867	-0.5	Dundee	14.763	-0.5
London Univ	204.750	+1.5	Edinburgh	44.143	-0.3
Imperial Coll	30.421	+1.2	Glasgow	44.220	-0.3
Loughborough	18.311	+2.1	Heriot-Watt	10.658	+0.4
Manchester Bus	1.101	-0.5	St Andrews	11.266	-0.4
Manchester	47.353	+1.7	Stirling	8.148	-0.5
UMIST	16.517	+1.4	Strathclyde	23.211	+1.8
Newcastle	31.819	-0.3	**Total Scotland**	**178.444**	**+0.5**
Nottingham	27.575	+1.5			
Oxford	44.244	0	**Total GB**	**1198.599**	**+1.0**
Reading	18.872	+0.1			
Salford	12.935	+1.1			

● Government funding for universities will fall by 2 per cent in real terms. The UGC calculates total cash increase of 3.1 per cent falls 2.51 per cent short of meeting projected inflation rate and growth of special university costs.

RESEARCH RANKINGS OF UK UNIVERSITIES

University	Top score	Bottom score	Average	University	Top score	Bottom score	Average
Cambridge	34	0	4.7	Exeter	1	1	2.9
Imperial	13	0	4.6	Glasgow	3	6	2.9
Oxford	32	0	4.6	Reading	1	1	2.9
UC London	20	0	4.3	St Andrew's	1	1	2.9
Warwick	11	0	4.1	Aberystwyth	0	1	2.8
LSE	7	0	4.0	Bath	0	1	2.8
Bristol	10	2	3.8	Leicester	1	2	2.8
UMIST	3	0	3.7	Swansea	1	3	2.8
York	3	0	3.7	Aberdeen	1	4	2.7
Manchester	3	0	3.6	Kent	2	3	2.7
Essex	5	0	3.4	Aston	1	2	2.6
Sussex	1	2	3.4	Loughborough	5	3	2.6
Edinburgh	7	5	3.3	Bangor	0	3	2.5
Liverpool	5	7	2.5				
Southampton	5	1	2.5				
Durham	3	4	2.5				
Lancaster	3	1	2.4				
Nottingham	7	10	2.4				
QMC London	1	11	2.3				
Sheffield	5	4	2.3				
Birmingham	3	5	2.2				
East Anglia	2	4	2.1				
Leeds	2	5	2.1				
Newcastle	2	5	2.0				
Birkbeck	2	8	2.0				
King's London	6	4	2.0				
Surrey	1						
Cardiff	2						

Number of departments with: Top score, Bottom score, Average

Source: UFC/FT

THE Universities' Fundi[…] research done in every [university] […] versities on a five-point […] […] of national excellence in

The first column show[s] […] each university's average ments given the top ran[k] […] departmental groupings, work of international e[xcellence] […] s," used by the Universi-plus national excellence […] […] to distribute its research
The second column shows the number of money.

Captions

1 The 1981 cuts
THES

2 The 1986-7 allocation
The Times, 21 May 1986

3 Research ranking 1989
Financial Times, 26 August 1989

4 Professor Kemp with the University's submission to the UFC

5 Award of the Carl Bertelsmann Prize 1990

I nward looking universities stagnate. Warwick has always sought to look outwards in its courses and in the 1980s, when it began to reach viable size, it has had a deepening impact on its local community and on the wider world. This impact is described in the following pages through research specifically orientated towards external needs, notably in industry, the creation of the Science Park as an agent of regional industrial regeneration, the establishment of the Arts Centre as a major cultural attraction, the opening of the University's facilities to community access, the development of continuing education, services to schools and the growth in international relationships. The University has benefited greatly from these activities. Its most significant impact on society must of course be through its graduates – more than 30,000 of them dispersed across every continent. In Britain they include MPs, journalists, industrialists, social workers, lawyers, bankers, teachers, artists, writers and musicians. They represent the ultimate test of the University's success.

Notes to the pictures will be found on page 121.

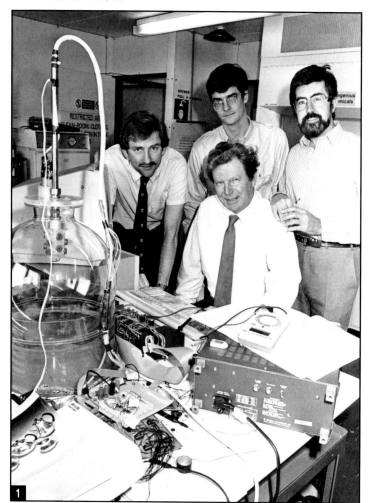

1   The Electronic Nose Team

2   The Biotransformations Group

3   Nanotechnology

4   Cancer Research

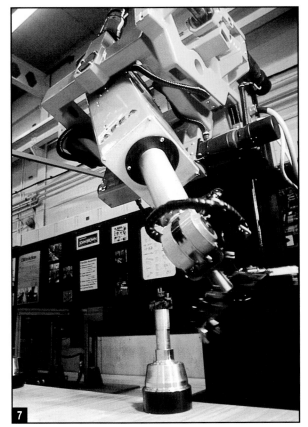

The Advanced Technology Centre, which is part of the Engineering Department, was opened by the then Prime Minister, Mrs Margaret Thatcher. The Centre is directed by Professor Bhattacharyya (shown above with the Prime Minister) and was financed by the Rover Group and Rolls-Royce.

The Barclays Venture Centre (above) was the first building on the Science Park and was designed as an 'incubator' for small high tech companies.

THE SCIENCE PARK

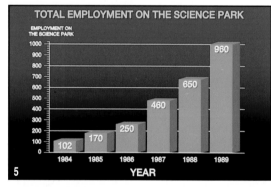

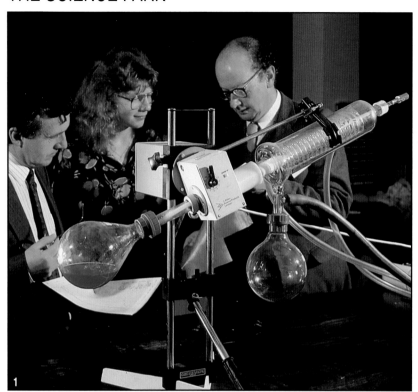

ANALYSIS OF TECHNICAL INTERESTS OF COMPANIES

- MECHANICAL AND ELECTRICAL ENGINEERING. — 8%
- CHEMISTRY AND MATERIALS. — 8%
- MEDICAL AND BIOTECHNOLOGY. — 6%
- INSTRUMENTS AND LAB EQUIPMENT. — 8%
- EDUCATION LINKED. — 6%
- OTHER. — 8%
- ELECTRONIC AND COMPUTER BASED MANUFACTURING SYSTEMS. — 30%
- OTHER ELECTRONIC SOFTWARE AND COMPUTER SYSTEMS. — 26%

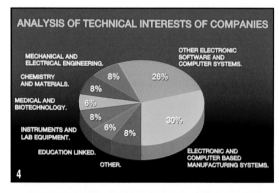

TOTAL EMPLOYMENT ON THE SCIENCE PARK

EMPLOYMENT ON THE SCIENCE PARK

YEAR	Employment
1984	102
1985	170
1986	250
1987	460
1988	650
1989	960

The distinctive feature of the Science Park is the close involvement of the University and the Science Park Board's insistence that companies must maintain a relationship with the University.

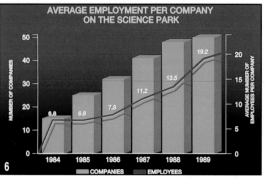

AVERAGE EMPLOYMENT PER COMPANY ON THE SCIENCE PARK

NUMBER OF COMPANIES / AVERAGE NUMBER OF EMPLOYEES PER COMPANY

6.8, 6.8, 7.8, 11.2, 13.5, 19.2

COMPANIES EMPLOYEES

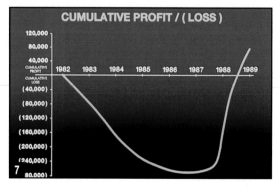

CUMULATIVE PROFIT / (LOSS)

CUMULATIVE PROFIT

CUMULATIVE LOSS

1982 1983 1984 1985 1986 1987 1988 1989

120,000 / 80,000 / 40,000 / (40,000) / (80,000) / (120,000) / (160,000) / (200,000) / (240,000)

CONTINUING EDUCATION

1 and 2   Open Studies classes

3   First graduating class of the Distance Learning MBA

4   CAD/CAM post experience course at Arden House

5   Radcliffe House

6   Shakespeare 6th Form Summer School

7   Chemistry 6th Form Summer School

8   Women into Science and Engineering (WISE) course in Computer Science

9   Warwick History Videos

10 Industrial placement for postgraduate student, organised by the Centre for Education
    and Industry

INTERNATIONAL

1   Signing an agreement with UNIN

2 and 3   The Namibia team

4   Negotiating an agreement in China

5   The Overseas University Management Programme

6   The University's Hong Kong office

1, 2, 3   Students in the Arctic, Zimbabwe, surveying in Turkey
4   Launch of Malaysian WGA
5   Poetry exchange with China

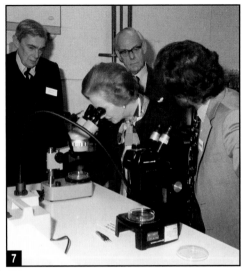

These statistics illustrate the growth and diversification of the University. Figures 1 and 2 highlight the effect of Government policies on student numbers in the early 1980s and the accelerated growth in the later 1980s. Figure 3 shows the growth in part-time student numbers. Figure 4 illustrates the growth in staff numbers, with the slow down in the early 1980s reflecting Government policies for those years, but a continuous rise in the numbers of research staff (who are funded externally through research grants and contracts). Figure 5 describes the sources of University income. The 1980s show UGC/UFC recurrent grant and home fees representing a falling proportion of the income with a very rapid growth in research income and in income from other sources. The statistics confirm Warwick's success in the 1980s – its increasing research activity, the diversification in its sources of income, and the overall growth in the size of the University.

STATISTICS

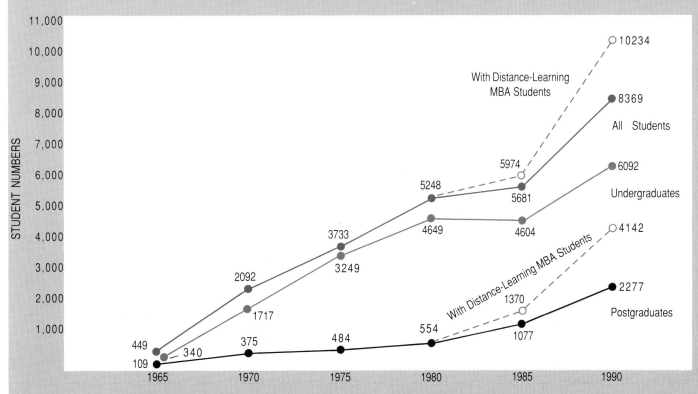

FIGURE 1 : STUDENT NUMBERS 1965 - 1990

Note: These numbers represent all students registered for degrees at the University, including part-time students, but excluding visiting and exchange students, and staff members registered for degrees.

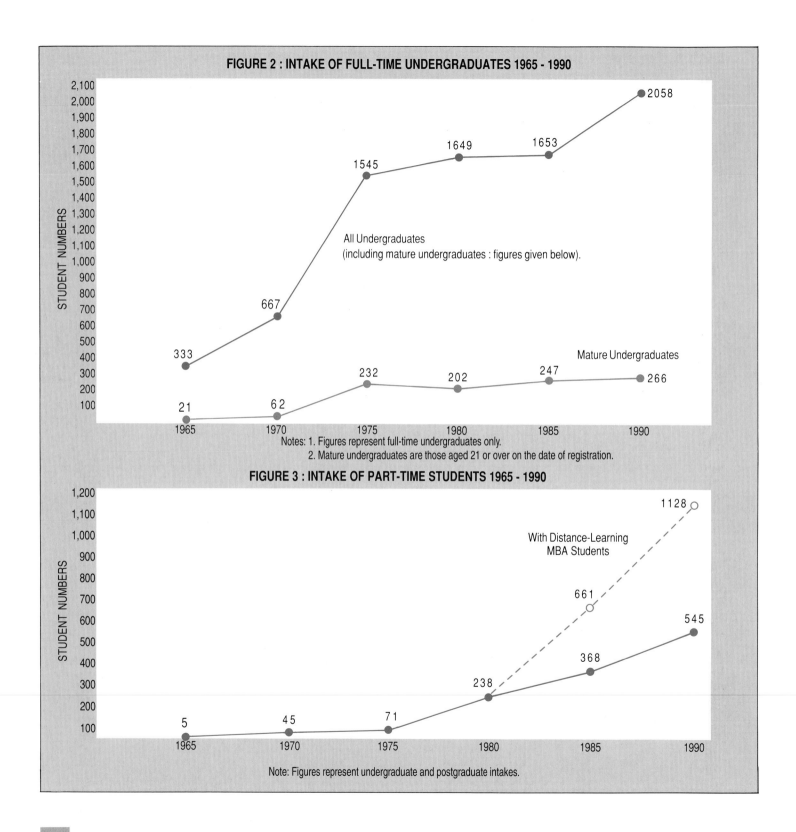

FIGURE 2 : INTAKE OF FULL-TIME UNDERGRADUATES 1965 - 1990

STUDENT NUMBERS

All Undergraduates
(including mature undergraduates : figures given below).

Mature Undergraduates

333
667
1545
1649
1653
2058

21
62
232
202
247
266

1965   1970   1975   1980   1985   1990

Notes: 1. Figures represent full-time undergraduates only.
2. Mature undergraduates are those aged 21 or over on the date of registration.

FIGURE 3 : INTAKE OF PART-TIME STUDENTS 1965 - 1990

STUDENT NUMBERS

With Distance-Learning
MBA Students

1128
661
545
238
368
5   45   71

1965   1970   1975   1980   1985   1990

Note: Figures represent undergraduate and postgraduate intakes.

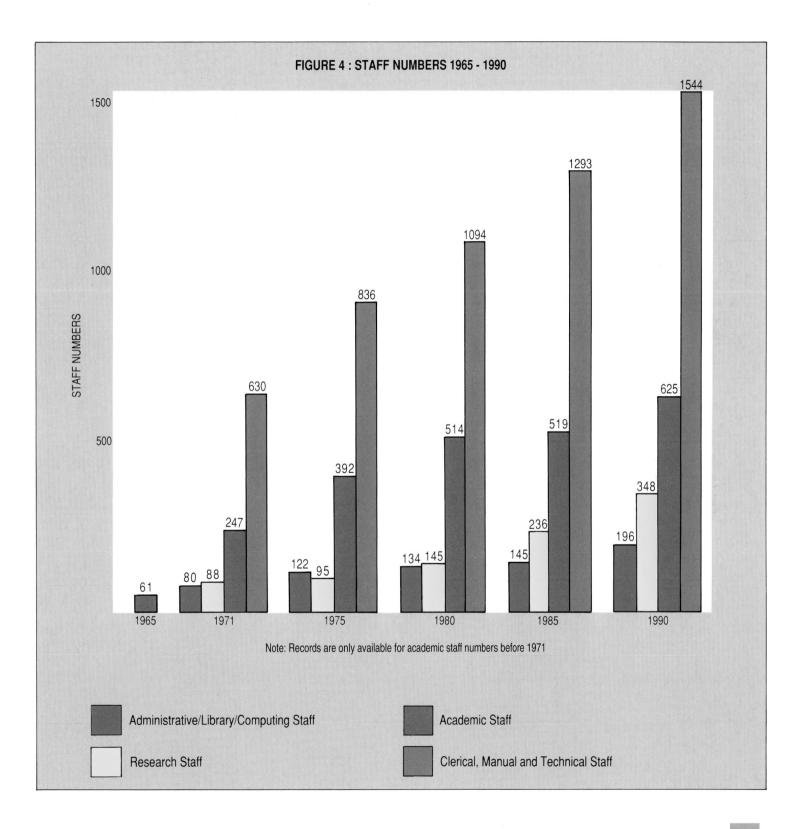

FIGURE 4 : STAFF NUMBERS 1965 - 1990

STAFF NUMBERS

Note: Records are only available for academic staff numbers before 1971

Administrative/Library/Computing Staff

Academic Staff

Research Staff

Clerical, Manual and Technical Staff

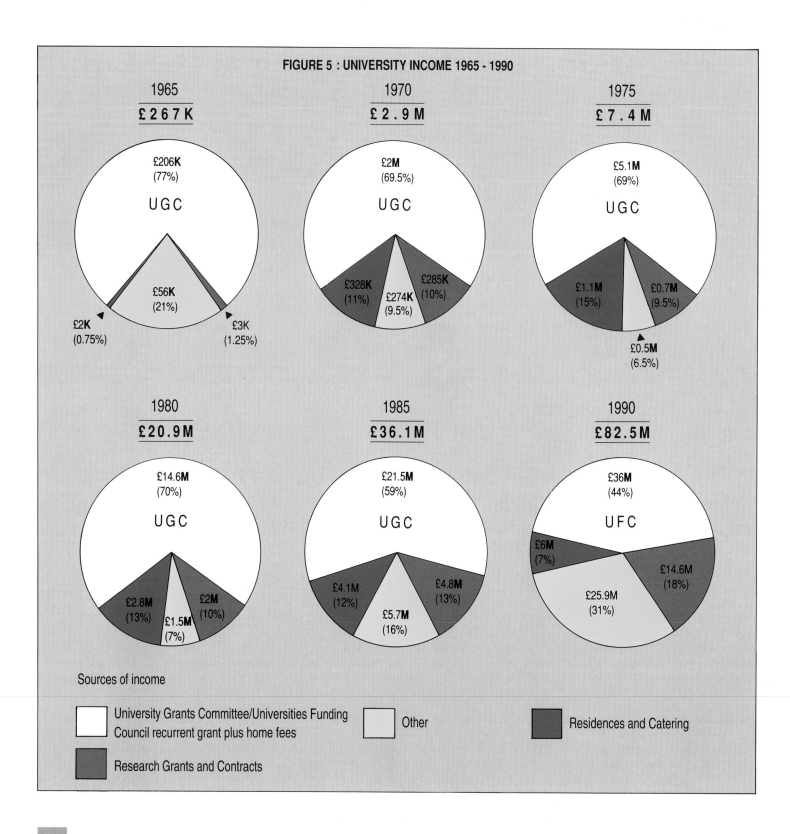

FIGURE 5 : UNIVERSITY INCOME 1965 - 1990

1965
£267K

£206K
(77%)
UGC

£56K
(21%)

£2K
(0.75%)

£3K
(1.25%)

1970
£2.9M

£2M
(69.5%)
UGC

£328K
(11%)

£274K
(9.5%)

£285K
(10%)

1975
£7.4M

£5.1M
(69%)
UGC

£1.1M
(15%)

£0.7M
(9.5%)

£0.5M
(6.5%)

1980
£20.9M

£14.6M
(70%)
UGC

£2.8M
(13%)

£1.5M
(7%)

£2M
(10%)

1985
£36.1M

£21.5M
(59%)
UGC

£4.1M
(12%)

£5.7M
(16%)

£4.8M
(13%)

1990
£82.5M

£36M
(44%)
UFC

£6M
(7%)

£25.9M
(31%)

£14.6M
(18%)

Sources of income

University Grants Committee/Universities Funding Council recurrent grant plus home fees

Other

Residences and Catering

Research Grants and Contracts

94

"Working and Researching at the Limits of Knowledge"

Robert G. Burgess

The 1960s was a period of educational expansion and development throughout the English school system and in higher education. Much of the development involved major building programmes: primary and middle schools, comprehensive schools, polytechnics and a variety of new universities. In the university sector there were seven new campuses developed on green field sites in England.[1] Warwick was among the last of the new universities, with over 400 acres on which to develop. Yet it was not just physical territory that was ripe for development, but also academic territory.

The opportunity is given to few vice-chancellors, professors and academic staff to develop a university from scratch, but this was the position for those in new universities. In the 1960s there was much discussion and debate about the strategies for university development, the structures of universities and the pattern of higher education through the publication of the Robbins Report,[2] and through the up-grading of Colleges of Advanced Technology to universities, the rise of the polytechnics, and the expansion of colleges of education.[3] But it was the new universities which provided the greatest opportunities as there were no buildings to inherit, no existing degree programmes to support and no staff. The shape and style of a university was there to be developed – a task that was taken on by the 'founding fathers' of the new universities. Some of the newly appointed vice-chancellors and their senior staff were quick to offer blueprints for new university development. The early sixties therefore witnessed a rash of conferences, papers and books which charted the developments of the new campuses.

The best known of these developments was at Sussex where Asa Briggs has argued they were redrawing the map of learning.[4] At Sussex, the basic academic unit was the multi-subject school – a development that has remained[5]. Here, inter-disciplinary work could be developed and disciplines could be linked. This became an important model for new universities where breadth of study was combined with depth – a pattern that was also taken up at East Anglia. At Kent, Lancaster and York, the collegiate system loomed large as the dominant university structure, while at Essex, key developments through the establishment of large departments were made known through the 1963 Reith Lectures given by Albert Sloman, their Vice-Chancellor.[6] At Warwick, there was relatively little publicly available comment on the development of the academic structure, or styles of teaching and patterns of learning on which staff in other new universities were writing. In contrast, Jack Butterworth, the Vice-Chancellor of Warwick, enunciated his views to staff and students when he claimed that his fundamental philosophy was to establish a university based on research, teaching and service to the community. His position involved giving the founding professors and their staff the opportunity to create the academic landscape: an opportunity that persuaded several people to come to Warwick rather than any of the other new universities. Professor Phillips-Griffiths (Griff), the founding professor of philosophy, summed up his feelings on new universities[7] (especially Sussex) and his reasons for coming to Warwick when he remarked:

> I didn't like the idea of the new university. And by the idea of a new university I thought Sussex. I didn't like anything about Sussex. On the other hand, if you go as a Chair to an established university you put up with whatever it is. Whereas being able to start your own department was tremendous. But I wouldn't have wanted to go to Sussex because I wouldn't be starting my own department. I would have been fitting into an academic and intellectual straitjacket at Sussex which was the last thing I wanted . . . When I discovered it was all wide open I agreed to come (to Warwick).[8]

These views were shared by other founding professors who were opposed to multi-subject schools and collegiate systems. They wished to develop their subjects and saw in Warwick the opportunity to establish subjects and departments. Yet this was different from the other new universities. In these circumstances, we need to ask: how did Warwick University develop? What structures were established? What patterns of teaching and learning were created? In short: how far did the initial strategy and key decisions shape the University in the first twenty-five years?

Starting points

The shape and style of many new universities was determined by the Academic Planning Boards, but at Warwick the situation was very different (see 'The Pre-history of the University' page 9). In an early meeting of the professors-elect in the academic year 1963-4, Jack Butterworth provided a two page paper on 'Academic Planning' in which he made it clear that the Board had not committed the University to any detailed academic plan. Instead, all academic developments were to be established by the professors on their appointment. The report of the Academic Planning Board to the University Grants Committee indicates how they envisaged Warwick would develop. In particular, they considered that the academic staff would develop their subjects and create a university community.

Subjects were to dominate Warwick – a clear message to the Vice-Chancellor and his founding professors. Furthermore, the Board gave a strong indication of the subjects they would like to see developed on the basis of demands for potential students and for which there was a career market. In particular, they wanted 'core' subjects to be developed 'in the humanities, English literature or history with an emphasis on the sociological and economic approach or in social studies, economics'.[9] In the humanities, their proposals were similar to other new universities and followed the fashion of the time where a degree course might be designed as follows:

Table 1: Proposed Humanities Degree Course[10]

Year I

1 Common University-wide Logic/Language Course
·
2 History
·
3 English Literature
·
4 Modern Language

Year II

1 History
·
2 Modern Language

Two options drawn from:

Economics
·
Geography
·
Archaeology
·
Sociology
·
Psychology

Year III

1 Dissertation (Historical or Literary Topic)
·
2 Documents/Texts in a chosen field

or the study of two cognate subjects.

Source: Based on Academic Planning Board paper on Academic Standards and Courses

Such a scheme gained little support among the founding professors as it was only Professor George Hunter in English who favoured

such a multi-disciplinary approach.

Meanwhile, in social studies the Academic Planning Board wanted a division into 'literates' and 'numerates'. The former would be based on a variation of the Oxford PPE (Philosophy, Politics and Economics) degree, while the latter was to involve a stream which would allow specialisation in economics and econometrics. In turn, it was hoped this combination would lead to an opportunity for graduate work and a graduate school of business studies (the latter being an idea encouraged once the Vice-Chancellor joined them). Finally, in science, the Board wanted to develop four basic subjects: mathematics, physics, chemistry and engineering given the costs of developing laboratory science. While the Academic Planning Board always wanted the Vice-Chancellor and the academic staff to map out the University, their plans did influence the choice of subject areas as they had to approve the fields in which founding professors were to be appointed: English, French and history in the arts; philosophy, politics and economics in social studies; and chemistry, mathematics and engineering in science. Furthermore, although the Board argued that the academic staff would set 'the shape and tone of the new university',[11] it is important to note that it favoured subjects being grouped in schools rather than in departments or faculties. On this basis, degree schemes would not follow the conventional single subject honours programme, but include a common first year course for all undergraduates. In his paper to the professors-elect, Jack Butterworth suggested that the main question to be addressed was how Schools of Studies and courses were to be organised. Nevertheless, the Vice-Chancellor and the professors-elect had been given several clues about academic development. Indeed, the Vice-Chancellor influenced the tone of the University by attempting to find founding professors from people who were considered the best in their subject. Some recall being approached at cocktail parties, others did not apply but were persuaded to come to Warwick on the recommendation of academic advisers, while some responded to public advertisements and recall being dined in Oxford and subsequently interviewed.

The kind of staff that Jack Butterworth wanted were those who saw a close link between teaching and research, a theme highlighted by the Robbins Report and discussed in several documents that were produced at Warwick. In an early report to the University Court, he remarked:

> Teaching and research in a university are complementary, for in the best university experience there is an intimate connection between research and teaching. Our students are taught by teachers who have regard to research, that is to say by teachers who are acquainted with the frontiers of their subject and teach with the attitude of a research worker.[12]

Certainly, this theme was to recur in several reports to the University Court when the Vice-Chancellor indicated that the work of a university was based on research which preceded the development of successful courses. This was not 'empty rhetoric' as the University developed a sabbatical leave scheme (one term after completing six teaching terms) when staff could conduct research on which much teaching was subsequently based. In a later report to Court the Vice-Chancellor stated:

> The essence of the university's activity lies in the intimate connection between teaching and research.

and continued:

> The distinctive thing about an undergraduate course is that students are taught by teachers who are either researchers or are acquainted with the frontiers of their subject.[13]

Indeed, even in his presentation to sixth formers on the University video in the mid-1970s, the Vice-Chancellor could be heard to tell them that the unique feature of a university lay in the fact that students were taught by academics who conducted research and who could take them to the 'very edge' of that subject. In this respect, Warwick's claim to be a research-led university which has produced high quality research and teaching in the 1970s and 1980s was present from the beginning.[14] While the Academic Planning Board wanted subjects to have a strong presence they also wanted a common course, and an academic structure based on schools and boards. But we might ask: how did these developments occur and how did they fare at Warwick in the 1960s?

An experiment at Warwick

The new universities were identified with innovation and change in higher education. Indeed, the experimental nature of new universities in general and Sussex in particular, was captured in a collection of essays subtitled 'An Experiment in Sussex'.[15] However, the situation at Warwick was very different from Sussex. Here, only one course was identified as an experimental scheme – namely the common first year course which had been advocated by the Academic Planning Board in the following terms:

> We are persuaded that irrespective of his bent every undergraduate in his first year should be taught (and examined in) language and logic, a course which we consider could be fruitful both academically and socially. To be able to think and write clearly and to examine one's relation to society (for we foresee that ethical examples would frequently be used in such a course) should prove a useful beginning in common in a new community and fulfil a need for all undergraduates, whether scientist or humanist, in their first year in a university.[16]

This course was taught under the title 'Enquiry and Criticism' and was described by one professor as 'Warwick's one great attempt to

innovate', while another claimed 'It was like all the professors giving inaugural lectures'. However, the task of planning this course was given to the Professor of Philosophy who considered it an opportunity to present to students a picture of the intellectual universe. He outlined his ideas in the following terms:

> What I thought of was a series. I called it 'Enquiry and Criticism' in that it seemed to me in the sciences particularly there was original enquiry where some other subjects, certainly literature, wasn't involved in writing novels and poetry creatively but in a critical understanding of a particular aspect of culture, and the same was true of French studies and so on. So that people were engaged in Enquiry and Criticism of it . . . and anyway it wasn't a bad sounding title.[17]

Before the course was given a title it went through several versions that were presented to meetings of the professors-elect. At an early meeting in 1963 they decided that a common course should be concerned with 'real issues' which would connect with students' interests and provide an opportunity for students to talk and write and encourage independence of mind. The proposed format included a course on sceptical problems devoted to the concept of knowledge, metaphysics, mathematics, common sense, natural sciences, social sciences, criticism, reason and conduct and education. This was to be followed by a second course entitled 'Logic and Language' that would focus on the nature of inference, the syllogism, recent logic and fallacies and thought and language.[18]

After a discussion of this proposal at a meeting of professors-elect in early January 1964 Phillips-Griffiths summarised the position that was reached:

> Many of those present thought that the suggestion made was one that might well be experimentally pursued; of these, one made criticisms of the content, and all agreed that some thought would have to be given to the method of instruction in the light of scarce teaching resources.[19]

The most fundamental criticism of course content came from Malcolm Clark (professor-elect in Molecular Sciences) who suggested the course was liable to produce 'nothing but a superficial froth'[20], while Christopher Zeeman (professor-elect in Mathematics) suggested ways in which the course could be restructured to avoid 'an undesirable emphasis on academic philosophy'[21]. There was also further debate on the use of lectures and seminars and whether lectures might be printed and distributed. It was considered that seminars would be difficult to organise, teach and find staff to take, given the range of subject matter involved. However, this course was not intended to introduce an interdisciplinary topic based around key themes, but rather to proceed 'according to the standards of an existing discipline'[22]. The intention was therefore to use philosophy as a discipline:

which could provide the sort of interdisciplinary interest required of a common course, while at the same time relying on accepted and disciplined standards of procedure.

However, Phillips-Griffiths continued:

> It will indeed not suffer from the kind of superficiality that some philosophy courses produce, since it will be deepened by the accounts of mathematicians and historians of what they themselves are doing . . .[23]

The course which eventually became 'Enquiry and Criticism' was proposed as a twenty-four week offering which included the following topics: the concept of knowledge (one week), the rationalist ideal (two weeks), the nature of mathematics (four weeks), common sense (one week), natural science (four weeks), social science (three weeks), literature and criticism (three weeks), reason and conduct (three weeks), and the aims of education (one week)[24].

This course was presented through one lecture and one seminar each week and was assessed by means of an essay of between 2,500 and 5,000 words that was written towards the end of the year. In the first prospectus for students entering Warwick in 1965 the course was said to be one:

> in which the methods of the various branches of knowledge such as mathematics, the natural and social sciences, literary criticism, ethics and politics, will be critically examined. Its aim will be to give the student a critical sense of the basis and limits of his own discipline, and of its place in the universe of knowledge.[25]

The lectures for this course were given in lecture theatre ELT I on the East Site and were followed by twenty-two parallel seminar group meetings. These seminars were conducted by group leaders who were responsible for chairing a discussion. All the seminar leaders were volunteers drawn from academic staff throughout the University. While some young lecturers found the material difficult to handle with the result that seminars were 'tough going', others could recall lectures from Christopher Zeeman on how exciting it was to be a mathematician, from George Hunter on how to criticise poetry, and from 'Griff' (Phillips-Griffiths) on moral problems. The style of the first course was summed up by Rolph Schwarzenberger (a seminar leader who was a Reader in mathematics at the time):

> What it [Enquiry and Criticism] was about was each professor trying to convince a general audience that his subject was an exciting thing to do; that's what it was about and by and large most of them did. I don't remember anything about the kind of material that I learnt. I don't think I learnt anything from the course. But what it did do was encourage me to respect links between departments and the

University. People sort of thinking: Yeah, that sounds quite interesting what those mathematicians do; I didn't realise mathematics was interesting and the same the other way round.

He continued:

> What came over very clearly was that in each subject area people go about it in different ways. How you might draw analogies between how a mathematician goes about it, how a philosopher goes about it. But I don't remember any attempt to create an overarching theory or anything like that. It wasn't a philosophy course.[26]

In many universities this course might have been presented as an interdisciplinary offering with links being made between different branches of knowledge. But at Warwick, the strength of subjects showed through as several professors used the lecture series to present the hallmarks of their disciplines and the ways in which they and other practitioners worked. This style of presentation lasted only one year and was followed in the second year by a shorter course of lectures in the first term which were presented by the professoriat and a second term where students took a specialist option on either probability, or problems of criticism or ethical and political thought or engineering. Once again, subject areas were dominant. However, this was the final year in which Enquiry and Criticism was organised as it became difficult to find volunteers from the staff to take the seminars, students were not required to

Students leaving the East Site, the main teaching area of the University in October 1965.

attend, and several students were permitted to take an alternative course. In addition, many staff argued that the new subject-based degrees required four discipline-based courses in the first year. Indeed, twenty five years later the basic structure of the Warwick first degree course consists of four courses in each year with a first year in which students can take an option outside the degree subject, but in many cases they are encouraged to stay within the boundaries of their chosen degree course. Subjects have always had a strong presence in the first year and Enquiry and Criticism was no exception as this course had a subject base. However, the strong subject base at Warwick resulted in this early experiment being abandoned without leaving an academic mark on the University – a situation that was later mirrored in the structure of schools and boards.

From Schools and Boards to Departments and Faculties

The Academic Planning Board had advocated subject schools being grouped into Schools of Studies rather than being organised in faculties. The idea of schools was a Sussex notion that encouraged cross fertilisation between a limited range of subjects. However, at Warwick, where professors had been appointed to develop subjects, it was widely regarded that each subject group was a department. Accordingly, several of the founding professors considered they had been given the opportunity to establish departments. Indeed, Dick Sargent (the founding Professor of Economics) claimed that because Jack Butterworth had given the professors the opportunity to develop their subjects:

> that was really why it grew up in this departmental way and that is why I think we always were a departmental university and so the nomenclature of schools and all that kind of thing was . . . a kind of fig leaf really.[27]

Certainly, the idea that the term 'schools' was a mere label to cover the organisation that staff regarded as a department was shared by others. For example, Christopher Zeeman commented:

> The great strength at Warwick lay in departments. Each department had a free hand to design its own syllabus, build its own building, recruit its own staff and students, and to set its structure up best for teaching and research.[28]

Similarly, Donald Charlton (the founding Professor of French Studies) commented:

> I thought of the School of French Studies as a Department of French Studies. I didn't care whether it was School or Department . . . I was never under any illusion.[29]

Each subject group was allocated to a School which was responsible for particular degree courses. In 1965-6 the Senate agreed that the composition of Schools of Studies should be as shown in Table 2:

Table 2: Composition of Schools of Studies		
School	**Membership**	**Degree Courses with which concerned**
1 Social Studies	All Economics All Politics Members of other subjects teaching for Degree Courses in the Schools (including Mathematics)	Economics A – D Economics F Politics and Economics
2 Historical Studies	All History All Politics All French All Philosophy Members of other subjects teaching for Degree Courses in the School	History History and Politics French Studies Philosophy Philosophy and Politics
3 Literature	All English All French Italian Members of other subjects teaching for Degree Courses in the School	English and European Literature French and European Literature English and American Literature
4 Engineering and Physics	All Engineering Science All Physics Representatives from Mathematics, Molecular Sciences and Economics	Engineering Science Physics Economics
5 Molecular Sciences	All Molecular Sciences Representatives from Mathematics and Physics	Molecular Sciences
6 Mathematics	All Mathematics Representatives from Economics, Engineering Science, Molecular Sciences, Philosophy and Physics	Mathematics (Pure)

Source: Paper on the Establishment of Boards of Studies and Schools of Studies for 1965-6

The Schools of Studies were regarded by several of the senior staff as broadly equivalent to a Sub-Faculty in other universities as they were responsible for the arrangements for undergraduate students and their courses and graduate students taking taught courses. The business for the Schools of Studies was to come from the subject groups for onward transmission to the Boards of Studies.

Some of the original staff recalled the way in which Schools of Studies were established at Warwick. In some cases it was argued that the groupings were artificial and contrived with little common purpose between the disciplines represented. This is well captured by Phillips-Griffiths who commented:

> We had to form Schools of Study, and philosophy went into the School of Historical Studies: French, history and philosophy. God knows why as we had no contact with them. Our greatest contact was politics at the early stage and we were in the School of Historical Studies which meant nothing, just time wasting. But in order to organise the University it had to be recognised that there were degrees in politics, degrees in philosophy and degrees in history, so you had a new institution that had never been known in the university before called subjects and there were chairmen and heads of subjects and what we'd got was a departmental system in which departments were called subjects running alongside this crazy Schools of Study thing. Then the Schools of Study disappeared and we had departments.[30]

In these circumstances, some staff recall how relatively little business was transacted in the Schools of Studies as discussion, debate and argument had taken place in the subject group. Accordingly, School meetings were recalled as short formal occasions in the presence of administrative staff.

All the Schools related to two Boards: the Board of Arts (originally called Humanities – but only in the initial plans and the first prospectus) and the Board of Science. The composition of the Boards of Studies in the academic year 1965-6 was as Table 3.

These Boards were responsible for all the teaching, research and curricula relating to the subjects attached to them and they were also responsible for graduate matters relating to students reading for higher degrees by research. However, some staff considered that Boards duplicated the work of Schools. Indeed, a paper by Alec Ford (a reader in economic history at the time) outlined some of the defects that were evident in the system by November 1966. In particular, he suggested that there was such duplication that the Board of Arts had little work to do. He also advocated converting the School of Social Studies into a Board of Social Studies. The result would be that some issues would be dealt with by subject groups who would be able to make direct recommendations to the Board of Social Studies. This was an early stage in the struggle to establish a separate Board of Social Studies – a situation that was achieved by October 1968 when a new Board came into existence with the following subject Schools assigned to it: economics,

Table 3: Composition of Boards of Studies in 1965-6	
1. Sciences	
Ex-officio: Vice-Chancellor	1
Ex-officio: Chairmen of Schools of Study	3
1 elected by each School	3
2 from each subject	10
Total	**17**

Subjects of the Board
Economics ■ Engineering Science ■ Mathematics
Molecular Sciences ■ Physics

2. Arts	
Ex-officio: Vice-Chancellor	1
Ex-officio: Chairmen of Schools	3
1 elected by each School	3
2 from each subject (except Italian)	14
Total	**21**

Subjects of the Board
Economics ■ English ■ French
History ■ Italian ■ Mathematics
Philosophy ■ Politics

Source: Paper on the Establishment of Boards of Studies and Schools of Studies for 1965-6

industrial and business studies, law, philosophy, politics and sociology (the latter being included when the School of Sociology was founded in 1970). Subsequently, in the early 1970s, the question of subject Schools and Boards was regularised by the Senate in their recommendations for revising the Charter and Statutes which were approved by the Privy Council and took effect from 1 October 1973. From that date, Boards of Studies became known as Boards of Faculties and most subject groups no longer used the term 'School', but instead took the title 'Department'; a situation that had unofficially operated in the University as a consequence of professors-elect being given the opportunity to establish their own disciplines. However, a Senate minute in June 1971 indicates that the introduction of the new titles was not to be regarded as amending the terms of reference of the bodies concerned. Indeed, if any subject School wished to use the title 'School' rather than 'Department' a case had to be submitted through the Faculty for consideration by the Senate. The first subject to use this procedure was the School of Law: it was permitted to use the title 'School' rather than 'Department' on a vote of nine to eight.

The strong department was the hallmark of the University of

Warwick as schools and boards were superfluous and faculties far less significant than departments. But how did subjects and departments operate? In what ways was subject dominance reflected in courses, in teaching programmes and research?

Establishing subjects

Statements from each of the founding professors in papers presented to the meetings of the professors-elect, descriptions in the university prospectus, and comments given to the local press, indicate that many professors had come to Warwick to establish a subject rather than an interdisciplinary school; the exception being George Hunter, the Professor of English.

Each professor started with a distinct view of his subject. In some cases they were reacting to the way it had developed elsewhere, in other cases there was a vision of a new perspective or a new orientation to their discipline, and how it could be developed given the encouragement of a Vice-Chancellor who had indicated they could develop subject areas. Among the statements provided by the founding professors, there were those who wished to reform the discipline (economics and history), those who wished to reform the teaching of the discipline (French studies and engineering), those who wished to compete nationally and internationally in research (mathematics) and one professor who wished to develop in an interdisciplinary way (English). It is to each of these developments that we now turn.

The School of Economics was founded by Dick Sargent who had decided to leave Oxford:

> partly due to a certain dissatisfaction with Oxford's institutional structure. In my experience the college system meant that (as far as humanities and social sciences were concerned) college tutors were rather isolated from their colleagues in the same subject. It seemed to me that opportunities to discuss one's subject (in my case economics) with one's subject colleagues were particularly necessary at a time of rapid development and increasing specialisation, and would be more likely to be found in a university which had a departmental rather than a collegiate structure.[31]

Such a view was very different from the Sussex model of interdisciplinary enquiry but fitted Sargent's notion of the development of his subject. In the early 1960s he had been on sabbatical leave in the USA where he had visited economists at the Massachusetts Institute of Technology and at Stanford. Here, he had been impressed with the willingness to innovate in such areas as econometrics, input-output analysis, linear programming and revision theory and so on. He saw there was greater specialisation among American economists who he considered had a more professional attitude to economics. Indeed, in an article entitled 'Are American Economists Better?' he concluded:

> A desire to treat the subject as if it were a discipline; eagerness to try out new techniques; willingness to specialise for the sake of the advancement of knowledge – all these things contribute to make American economists professionally better than ourselves.[32]

However, it was difficult to develop economics at Oxford where it was one of three subjects (in PPE) and where it lacked depth. Accordingly, he saw that Warwick provided the opportunity to establish the subject in a way whereby technical competence would be required in analytic tools, and where statistics and mathematics would have a major role. Once appointed, he argued that a second professorship was required in mathematical economics – a post to which Graham Pyatt was appointed. Pyatt identified the significant features of the development of economics at Warwick in the following terms:

> Dick Sargent made it clear from the outset that economics would have mathematics as part of the first year syllabus and that the teaching would build on that foundation. Now this was something that was very important for the development of economics, particularly at that time. I mean, we take it for granted much more these days than we used to, but at that time it was a brave and important step that immediately differentiated Warwick's economics from the other new universities.[33]

This was an important development for Warwick economics which has always had a highly quantitative orientation even in areas such as the study of economic history.

Similarly, in the Department of History, John Hale (the founding professor) had a vision of his subject that was different from other universities. The emphasis was well summarised in the *Coventry Evening Telegraph*:

> The history syllabus will concentrate on breadth rather than on chronological completeness. The emphasis will be on Europe and America, and England will be treated as a European country and will not be given especially detailed treatment. The aim of the syllabus is to provide a sound and uninsular historical training which appeals to the imagination.[34]

In addition, the course was to include periods of study in America and in Italy. The latter is still a distinctive feature of the degree programme as generations of history students (and subsequently history of art students) at Warwick have had the opportunity to study in Venice. However, a major feature of the degree was the initial focus on the Modern period. Alastair Hennessy (who was initially appointed to a senior lectureship in history) remarked:

> The real originality of the degree was what I call chrono-

logical inversion. We had the view that what happens in school is that you start in the year 1400 and by the time you come to university you probably, if you're lucky, get up to the nineteenth century so you have none of the background. We had this tremendous feeling of how history had to be relevant.[35]

The pattern that developed in the early years at Warwick was a first year course that commenced with the French Revolution and focussed on the Modern period before returning to studies of the Early Modern period. Subsequently, history courses have developed in particular streams: Renaissance and Modern; Modern European; and European and American. Common to all these degree schemes is Basic History which all students are required to take. This was an original aspect of the initial degree programme as the department perceived of the Atlantic as a totality. In this sense, the subject area broke new ground when established at Warwick.

Meanwhile, in French Studies, Donald Charlton had a distinct view of the way in which the teaching of the discipline could be reformed. His conception of the teaching of French departed from establishing the conventional degree scheme in French language, literature and philosophy. Instead he focussed on:

> French studies in which students did modern language and some literature. But they also had to do from a choice, French history periods, French politics and then we added to it sociology, art and cinema . . . If you look at the first prospectus you will see the list is relatively short.[36]

This conception of combining French culture, literature and civilisation was regarded by several staff as a form of 'French Greats'.

Here, a distinctive feature was not to use exclusively members of the French department but to draw on specialists from other departments to contribute particular courses. For example, Malcolm Anderson (then Senior Lecturer in Politics) taught a course in French politics and institutions, while members of the History department offered courses in different periods of French history. As a consequence, Charlton considered that he was only recruiting part of the team to establish French Studies. This allowed him to focus on providing specialists in language, literature and French thought, while drawing historians, political scientists and others from subjects elsewhere in the Board of Arts – a trend that is mirrored in the single and joint honours degrees in French Studies that are provided in 1990. These services were not given free by the subjects involved: at an early stage Graham Pyatt and Christopher Zeeman devised a method of counting full time equivalent student numbers called 'the matrix' on which staffing allocations to subjects were subsequently based.

Similarly in the field of engineering, Arthur Shercliff (the founding professor of Engineering) was concerned with the way the subject would be taught. In a paper to the Professors Elect he commented:

> It is perhaps necessary at the outset to correct a few popular fallacies. Engineering courses are commonly expected to impart a miscellany of useful facts which should enable an engineer to practise his profession. This may be true of medical training, but it should not be true of an undergraduate engineering science course. An engineering science school should aim primarily to produce in students an attitude of mind, a confident, critical, appraising and sometimes sceptical attitude towards physical situations and industrial practices which is based on a sound knowledge of fundamentals and an active imagination. We really ought to call our Engineering School the 'School of Well-informed Common Sense'.[37]

In particular, he was not concerned with how much material could be taught in the three year programme as he considered that much of it would be out of date within ten years. Accordingly, he considered that:

> Engineering courses should endeavour to teach less, not more, and to use the opportunity thereby created, to make sure that what *is* taught is really absorbed by the student to the point where he can use it creatively so that he can later face the ever increasing range of fresh problems with confidence and competence.[38]

Engineering students at Warwick were not to be trained for 'immediate entry into a particular technology', but were encouraged to focus on 'some stimulating intellectual activity'. In short, Arthur Shercliff was a great advocate of a unified Engineering department. However, when courses in engineering science did not take off to the extent that had been expected, he broadened and sharpened his concept of engineering by providing the opportunity to take it with another subject and to engage in specialist branches of engineering within a general department. Yet he was also pioneering in another sense as he attempted to attract more women students into the subject. Indeed, Michael Hughes (who was originally appointed as a Lecturer in Engineering) recalled one-third of the first student intakes being women students[39].

Meanwhile, professors in some subject areas considered that they were involved in developing a research-led enterprise which would have the potential to compete for staff and graduate students nationally and internationally; a situation that was reflected in mathematics. In common with other founding professors, Christopher Zeeman's plans were partly formulated in the context of attempting to reform the subject in his own university (in this case Cambridge) and partly as a reaction to what had occurred in establishing subject groups in other new universities (especially Sussex). Zeeman considered it was:

extremely important to set it (mathematics) up orientated towards research, as I had seen other new universities wait four years to get their own students for research degrees and by that time the whole department had solidified towards an undergraduate orientation rather than research. If you solidify towards a research orientation then the under-graduate orientation will happen anyway because you've got to teach undergraduates.[40]

He acted on this initial plan by bringing some research students with him from Cambridge in October 1964, one year ahead of the first undergraduates. For Zeeman, the strength of the subject could be established through strong individual subjects in mathematics: topology, algebra and analysis. The result was the potential to establish a graduate programme, a taught Master's course and a modern syllabus at undergraduate level which were all supported by research orientated staff rather than individuals who merely provided teaching. The notion of Warwick as a university whose subject areas were to be research-led was writ large in mathematics which has developed and sustained a world class reputation over twenty five years.

Yet there was also another view which was popular in other New Universities but which had relatively little influence or support at Warwick; namely, multi-disciplinary and interdisci-plinary work. Among the founding professors it was only Professor George Hunter who wanted to develop in this way. His vision was captured in the statement provided on English in a special issue of the *Coventry Evening Telegraph* in 1965 in which it was stated:

> The central aim of the course in English, and of the School of Literature as a whole, is to teach people to read with enjoyment and with an understanding of their enjoyment; and to stretch this capacity to cover as wide a range of literature as possible.
>
> The academic tradition that separates one national litera-ture from another has not been accepted; the ability to understand and enjoy a Shakespeare play is not different in kind from the capacity to enjoy and understand a translation of a novel by Dostoievsky or play by Brecht.
>
> As England is not a country existing by itself, so English will be studied in Warwick in the context of other literature, this can be either European or American.
>
> The assumption that only when literature is enjoyed can it be understood has determined the selection of books for close study. Only the best in world literature is good enough to remain continuously alive in the reader's mind when sub-jected to intense scrutiny.[41]

Here greater emphasis was placed on literature in general rather than English in particular, thus signalling a commitment to multi-disciplinary study, an academic organisation based on the then fashionable idea of schools, and the complete antithesis of the plans

of the Professor of French. While early copies of the prospectus made reference to degree courses using subject titles it was only English that used the title School of Literature which it was claimed was:

> designed to provide a framework of basic literary texts of common importance to all modern literatures, and to study a core of national literature, history and thought within this framework.[42]

Only at postgraduate level was English listed as a separate subject[43], but even here it was indicated that the School of Literature provided opportunities for advanced study in English, American and European literature. At this level, minor authors were intro-duced to students during their MA year – a course that it was argued was appropriate for approximately a quarter of the students admitted to the university. In this respect, the Sussex model was strongly mirrored here if not elsewhere at Warwick. However, it was unlikely to take root and flourish, given the extent to which all the other professors were developing their subjects and in turn departmental structures in all but name. Donald Charlton remarked:

> The founding professors wanted single subject degrees involving a redefinition of their own discipline. It follows from that, that the root reality of Warwick's academic organisation was going to be departments.[44]

This was a widely shared view among the professors-elect, but how did they set about building departments?

A range of Warwick's early prospectuses.

Creating Departments

We have already seen how many of the founding professors saw Warwick as a departmental university, but how did they set about staffing subject areas? Each founding professor went about it in a slightly different way: some built up a small group from professor to assistant lecturer (mathematics), others bid for a further chair (economics and molecular sciences). Nevertheless, they were all agreed that they were looking for the best staff they could find – an identical strategy to that followed by Jack Butterworth in making their own appointments. The way in which individuals were appointed also revealed a similar style: some could recall no application or interview – merely an invitation to join a subject group, while others applied to public advertisements and found themselves interviewed in Gonville and Caius College, Cambridge (in the case of molecular scientists). However, in these instances, the interview consisted of a conversation over a cup of coffee rather than questions from a specially structured committee which constituted later appointment panels.

This was a time of opportunity. In the words of one newly appointed assistant lecturer, it appeared that 'the sky was the limit' at Warwick. Even for those who were appointed to more senior positions there was great opportunity as they were told they were being promoted ahead of their time on the basis of research potential. This was the 1960s when expansion and excitement were available to university staff. The spirit of the time is well captured by Graham Pyatt who explains the context in which opportunities were provided for younger people:

> The situation in economics was really quite unique at that time because there had been . . . the expansion of the new universities and my generation was therefore fortunate to find itself in the situation where universities had one of two choices. They could either go for older people who had been passed over the first time round or they could go for younger people and so myself and a number of my contemporaries – many of us from Cambridge, which was a very lively place in economics in those days – were given the opportunity of being considered for chairs much sooner than we expected.[45]

This was the context in many subjects where the tendency was to appoint younger people.

In some subject areas, the founding professor established a group of staff from assistant lecturer to reader. This was the case in mathematics, where Christopher Zeeman developed the idea of establishing a department around a series of groups. He remarked:

> I thought if you're going to be internationally competitive in recruiting research students, you've got to be strong in individual subjects so the best thing would be to have the first six posts in the geometry/topology area, the second six posts in the algebra area, the third six posts in the analysis area, the fourth six posts in the applied area.[46]

Here the tactic was to appoint a professor with one or two readers who would go ahead and recruit lecturers and assistant lecturers who could compete in the international market. The way in which the first group was established was recalled by Rolph Schwarzenberger:

> Well, there's a myth and then there is the reality. The myth is that Zeeman wrote to six people and said, 'All the other five have accepted, will you come as well?'. The reality was that I heard he had been appointed, I wrote and congratulated him. He said, 'Oh, I've got some interesting ideas like not doing applied maths', and I wrote back and said, 'That sounds great' and I was more or less offered the job. No, I wasn't looking for a job in a new university and all other new universities were not attractive to a mathematician, and anyway I was very happy at Liverpool. Christopher's way of putting it was 'We've got the money to offer you a readership several years ahead of when you could possibly get it at Liverpool'.[47]

In this way, the topology group was steadily assembled after which an algebra group was established with Sandy Green as the professor and Roger Carter as a reader who then selected the other four staff to join them.

Some subject groups developed in a different way. For example, engineering had to appoint a number of people whose expertise was thinly spread across a very broad subject field. The result of such a policy was recalled by Michael Hughes in engineering when he remarked:

> Staff meetings consisted of Arthur [Shercliff] designating in quotes 'experts' on various problems that came up. I remember I drew the short straw on patents. I was for a short while the department's expert, so called, on patents, although my knowledge of patents could have been easily written on the head of a pin. Everybody on the staff also had an expectation that they would work to get membership of national committees and so on.[48]

He also indicated that the members of this subject group were also all expected continually to submit proposals to the then Science Research Council and to industry in an attempt to gain support for their ideas and to convince others that they could be taken seriously. As far as industrial links were concerned, encouragement was given to work with and for companies in the 1960s and 1970s. However, such work was based, according to Michael Hughes, on 'foot in the door stuff' – a far cry from subsequent developments in manufacturing in the 1980s when close links were established with major companies by a very powerful Department of Engineering. Clearly, this was a different way of establishing a science depart-

Table 4: University Staff – February 1966								
Subject	Professors	Readers	Senior Lecturers	Lecturers	Assistant Lecturers	Associate Professors	Research Fellows	TOTAL
Economics	2	1		2	2			7
Business Studies	1							1
Industrial Relations	1							1
English	1			5	1			7
French	1	1	1	1	4	1		9
History	1	1	1	2	3			8
Philosophy	1			2	3			6
Politics	1		2	1	2			6
Engineering Science	2	1	1	4		1		9
Mathematics	2	3		5			1	11
Molecular Sciences	2	2		2	5	3	13	27
Physics	1	1		3			6	11
TOTALS	16	10	5	27	20	5	20	103

Source: Based on numbers in the University Graduate Prospectus 1966-7.

ment – a situation that was partly a consequence of the subject matter.

One feature of this expansion programme developed by Zeeman and by Shercliff concerned departmental size, as the idea was to establish a critical mass in each subject area (see Table 4). Similarly, staff in molecular sciences also had plans to be a large department. Indeed, even before the university opened it was claimed that the School of Molecular Sciences would have a staff of ten professors and five associate professors by the early 1970s[49]. In fact, by February 1966 the School had a staff of twenty-seven[50]. The numbers in Molecular Sciences (largely boosted by associate professors and research fellows) gave rise to accusations of empire building – a theme which was also reflected in debates on resources, course structures and research activities. However, it was not just in science where curriculum discussion and debate occurred, as in other areas, staff were concerned to construct a first degree curriculum – a topic that is seldom discussed in higher education.[51]

Constructing courses and admitting students

From the very early days the Warwick development plan indicated that the 'founding fathers' had considerable ambitions. In the first plan published in 1964 student numbers were forecast in terms of 5,000 by the mid-1970s and the projections were made for 10,000, 15,000 and almost 20,000 students. Certainly, it was made clear to the professors-elect that expansion was to be rapid in the early years. A paper prepared by the Registrar for the meeting of the professors-elect in January 1964 demonstrates that Warwick was to focus on postgraduate as well as undergraduate students. The estimated student numbers are shown in Table 5 on page 106.

In practice, Warwick had 3,274 students by 1975 but greatly expanded in 1978 when a merger occurred with the Coventry College of Education which resulted in a fourth faculty and a student total of 5,013. By October 1990 the University had over 8,000 full-time and part-time students, with almost 2,000 more on distance-learning programmes (see page 91). While the subject matter has changed, the basic structure of single and joint honours degrees at undergraduate level, taught masters programmes and research degrees is the basic mixture that was developed in the mid-1960s.

When the University opened in 1965 teaching activities were concentrated in eighteen undergraduate degree courses. Twenty-five years later in October 1990 there were ninety-eight full-time undergraduate courses and a part-time degree programme. At postgraduate level there were nine MA/MSc programmes available in 1965 and opportunities to study for the degrees of MPhil and PhD in ten subject areas (although mathematics and engineering registered PhD students in 1964). In contrast, the postgraduate

Table 5: Proposed Student Numbers 1965 – 1974											
		1965	1966	1967	1968	1969	1970	1971	1972	1973	1974
Under-Graduate	Intake	300	400	550	700	800	950	1100	1250	1400	1550
	Total	300	700	1250	1650	2050	2450	2850	3350	3750	4200
Graduate Courses	Intake				45	60	85	105	120	145	165
	Total				45	80	150	150	175	205	240
Research	Intake	20	15	15	45	60	80	105	120	140	165
	Total	20	30	40	75	120	185	245	305	365	425
TOTALS		320	730	1290	1770	2250	2785	3245	3830	4320	4865

Notes:
1. These numbers excluded Education students. 2. The numbers included the proportions of postgraduate students envisaged by the Robbins Report in 1963.

Source: Expansion Programme paper by A. D. Linfoot (Registrar), January 1964.

prospectus for those students wishing to enter Warwick in October 1990 provides fifty-eight taught courses for the degrees of MA, MBA, MEd and MSc through full-time and part-time study, and a distance learning MBA, while thirty-eight subject areas provide MPhil and PhD supervision.

The undergraduate programmes that were developed were all honours and joint honours degrees. In the arts and social studies areas, the common pattern was to have four courses each year in which students were given the opportunity to specialise in depth. In the sciences, all the founding professors had been recruited from Cambridge. Together they planned a joint first year which was similar to the Cambridge natural sciences, but after a while this floundered as each subject area wanted a larger percentage of the time available and they also wanted 'matrix credit' from student numbers to expand staff. The distinctive characteristic of all Warwick degrees has been the strong subject orientation taught through lectures, seminars and tutorials as the teachers have wanted, like the founding professors, to establish close contact with their students. The Warwick teaching pattern marked it out from teaching and learning in other parts of the university system in the UK.

The Warwick single honours degrees had a central core which set out the essential features of a discipline. The joint honours programmes were established between many subject areas. The way in which these programmes were developed is well summarised by Professor Phillips-Griffiths who remarked:

One should only go into this sort of thing (joint degrees) where you can actually make sense of a joint degree not only when the subjects are complementary, but where there is an area between the two subjects that certain minds can inhabit and this was easy in philosophy and politics because half of politics is what used to be political philosophy in philosophy.

He continued:

The thing that worked best was philosophy and literature. The idea was a really integrated degree where two subjects confident of what they were doing in their own right should co-operate and the teachers should be such that they could not only expect the students to make something of this as an integrated degree, but they could teach the students in the same room at the same time.[52]

This is the hallmark of many of the joint degree programmes where subject areas moved into uncharted territory to create not only a joint degree, but joint teaching programmes which became core courses in each year – the result was a set of integrated programmes in joint honours degrees. Yet there were areas where difficulties arose when so-called joint degree courses were not well integrated because the founding professors and members of their subject groups had different aims.

In some areas of the University, such as the Board of Arts, attempts were made to establish joint degree programmes which would contribute to multi-disciplinary and interdisciplinary study. A joint working party of the Schools of Historical and Literary Studies (chaired by Fred Reid (a Lecturer in History) in 1969) acknowledged that some interdisciplinary teaching was conducted at Warwick in degrees in one subject school. However, much interdisciplinary activity appeared to the working party to occur in joint degrees where one or two joint directors of these degrees were required to maintain communication with subject schools and students so that problems could be resolved easily. Nevertheless, it was their view that genuine interdisciplinary work depends upon 'intimate teaching collaboration, based upon mutual trust and respect between the teachers involved'.[53] Alastair Hennessy considered that the distinction could be drawn between multi-disciplinary activities in two subjects where the student had to make the link between those subjects and interdisciplinary activity where links were made by the teaching staff. He commented:

> With interdisciplinarity you have joint teaching and you really do come to grips with what are the constraints and imperatives between two particular disciplines, which is difficult because it does presuppose like minded people.[54]

However, he considered that such interdisciplinary activity had to be worked at within Warwick given the disappearance of Schools of Studies within a few years of the University opening and the development of very entrenched departments. As well as joint degrees with joint teaching programmes, the University's interdisciplinary teaching activities were also developed through the idea of joint schools such as Comparative American Studies where staff from a range of subject areas – history, literature, politics and languages – focus on the study of history and culture in the United States, Canada, the Caribbean and Central and South America. Indeed, in the Faculty of Arts, joint schools have also developed in classics and ancient history, film and literature and also theatre studies.

Despite these developments, there were still some areas where no joint programmes were established. For example, in the arts there were no joint programmes in English and history or English and French – a situation which Alastair Hennessy considered was the result of the work staff were doing. He remarked:

> In setting up a university one spends a hell of a lot of time on meetings and the rest of it, and I think we all felt that what we were doing was too interesting and too exciting and we didn't want to get snarled up with all these things and with trying to iron out differences with other departments.[55]

Meanwhile, in the sciences there was concern over the territory that was being colonised by molecular sciences. In this area, Malcolm Clark, the founding professor, had a very special view of chemistry. According to Terry Kemp (an assistant lecturer in 1965 but now a professor of chemistry):

> Malcolm had been very impressed that the biggest growth in biology came about through the Watson-Crick model and he knew Crick, of course, being in Cambridge, and he felt that the major problems facing science in the last half of the twentieth century were going to be in the area of biology, and therefore he saw the need to train people who, while having a basic chemical training, could think both in terms of enzyme systems and molecular biology in general and also in terms of crystallography. So what made it different was a much larger chunk of crystallography than was in any other degree course anywhere and also a very large chunk of biochemistry, and all the students did this degree course

called molecular sciences which was 50% chemistry, 15% crystallography, 35% biochemistry and it was really unique in its time.[56]

Such a programme eventually had problems in recruiting sixth form students who did not identify with molecular sciences and who did not recognise the way in which the subjects they had studied at school and college related to this degree course. In addition, there were also problems with colleagues who were concerned about the all embracing nature of molecular sciences which claimed to include molecular physics at one extreme and molecular biology at the other. Some staff can still remember the famous printer's error in the university undergraduate prospectus in 1968-9 which stated that molecular sciences covered 'the broad spectrum of chemistry, from molecular physics to molecular physics'.[57] Although only a printer's error, it had considerable symbolic significance as it suddenly reduced the vast scale of molecular sciences in a very public setting.

In the late 1960s and early 1970s, biological sciences staff worked alongside colleagues in molecular sciences whose teaching and research was said to run:

> from theoretical chemistry and crystal structure analysis through spectroscopy and synthetic studies to biochemistry and molecular biology.[58]

The result was that the first Professor of Biological Sciences started off within a biological sciences division of molecular sciences. Indeed, some of the undergraduate prospectuses of the early 1970s indicate that biological sciences was a division of molecular sciences until October 1972 when biological sciences became a separate department. This was a result of disagreements about the way in which the area should develop. When biological sciences became a separate department with its own biochemists, several staff considered this situation was significant for molecular sciences as the original conception could not survive with biochemists in two different departments.

Such boundary disputes occurred in other parts of the University and were considered by some staff to be a direct consequence of the Vice-Chancellor's policy of giving founding professors the right to establish their subject areas. However, disputes also occurred when areas that were initially designed by others were subsequently taken over by professors who were appointed to develop a 'new' subject field. For example, some of the territory included in business studies was closely associated with economics in the early days of the University. As early as March 1965, Dick Sargent, the founding Professor of Economics, was writing in the *Coventry Evening Telegraph* about the ways in which education for management could be developed at Warwick[59]. He demonstrated that the University was in a favourable position to develop education for management, given that endowments had been obtained to establish professorships in business studies and industrial relations alongside other appointments in social studies which would allow teaching and research to be developed from different perspectives. He proposed a one year postgraduate Master's programme which would be built around techniques of quantitative analysis, operational research, organisational theory and the sociology of industry together with courses in industrial relations, economic policy, accounting and marketing. Meanwhile, it was envisaged that a Professor of Business would have as a specific responsibility the development of case histories of business experience that could be used in courses for middle management.

In the graduate studies prospectus for 1966-7 the course that Sargent had outlined was included as an MA in business studies and incorporated in the entry for economics. In addition, the staff list for economics also included the Professors of Industrial Relations and Business Studies. However, the Professor of Business Studies had come to Warwick with the idea of establishing a separate school as he did not approve of the ways in which business studies had been developed in other institutions, such as the ex-CATs and the civic universities, which had developed this area out of departments of engineering and economics. At Warwick, the idea was to establish a business school around four subject areas: economics and accounting, quantitative methods, engineering technology of business and the behavioural sciences. These areas were reflected in the courses on offer in 1967-8 at graduate level: an MSc in management and business studies for students who wished to develop a career in management, and an MSc in management science and operational research for students who wished to study problems in management. Both degree programmes provided courses on industry as a social institution, functional fields of management, the economic environment, integrative studies and quantitative methods (although there was more quantitative work in the management science and operational research course). At this time, teaching was conducted by staff drawn from business studies and economics.

An Engineering Science project in the laboratory.

However, business studies gradually acquired specialists in the 1970s and flourished in the 1980s with a research-led programme focussed on a variety of MBA degrees and other courses of advanced study. Much of the research was located in research centres which had been a feature of the Warwick landscape from the 1960s and to which we now turn.

Teaching and research

A dominant theme in the development of the University has been the close relationship between teaching and research and between teaching, research and service to the community. In this respect, the first Vice-Chancellor argued that teaching is dependent upon research, and research derives benefit from the researcher being engaged in teaching. At Warwick, this balance has been achieved through the creation of research centres which in a disciplinary based university has facilitated the development of many inter-disciplinary activities. These centres, units and institutions have also conducted work on behalf of the local community. One of the areas in which this type of development occurred was in the field of industry where Professors Clegg and Sargent proposed that a Centre for Industrial Studies should be established where university staff could 'make a contribution to the systematic analysis of industrial problems.'[60] This Centre was to be concerned with industrial relations, industrial economics and industrial sociology where it was argued university teachers would work alongside research assistants who would be involved in the day-to-day work associated with data collection in local firms. The projects which would be taken on would not only be defined by members of the University, but also by those engaged in industry. In this respect, it was envisaged that such a Centre would bring the University and the community closer together through teaching and research activities. In order to bring about a close inter-relationship between teaching and research it was argued that:

> Members of the staff of the Centre for Industrial Studies should be required to take part in the teaching of· the University; in the undergraduate schools or in the courses in management education, according to their particular qualifications and interests. They would also take part in the supervision of the research students in the field of industry, whom the establishment of the Centre should attract. In this way it would make a contribution to the costs of the University and also dispose it towards helping to finance the further expansion of the Centre. At the same time the facilities of the Centre should be available to the ordinary teaching staff of the University – both those concerned with undergraduate work and those concerned with management education – who have particular pieces of research work that they wish to undertake in the field of business and need assistance with the collection and preparation of data, computing, secretarial work and so on. Arrangements should be

evolved whereby members of the University staff might be seconded to the Centre for limited periods, for advanced study and research; and it would be particularly valuable if these could be extended to people from industry, somewhat along the lines of the opportunities which now exist at the Universities of Manchester and Oxford for senior civil servants.[61]

In 1965 this was a proposal which was subsequently developed in greater detail by Professors Clegg and Pyatt, who became the joint directors of the Centre for Industrial Economics and Business Research (CIEBR).

In this particular Centre there was an opportunity to bring together staff from economics and business studies who could develop work which would be of relevance to British management and that would draw on fields such as mathematical economics, marketing and operational research. In these areas, it was considered that insufficient work was being developed in Britain, with the result that Graham Pyatt argued:

> the desire was to get a research component into business studies and to bridge the gap with economics most immediately because that was the obvious source potentially for a lot of the tools that might be needed.[62]

However, there was also to be a two way flow with economists bringing their techniques to bear on problems that preoccupied people in business studies. The result was an umbrella organisation where teachers could be joined by researchers who would be funded by outside organisations. In this way, the Centre proved to be a catalyst for establishing research in an area and for getting research work done. Such was the strength of this Centre that it in turn sponsored further Centres – the Industrial Relations Research Unit and the Institute for Employment Research – that both have a strong place in the Faculty of Social Studies in the 1990s.

Similarly, in all the other faculties in the University, research centres are a strong feature of the landscape. In mathematics, Christopher Zeeman established the Mathematics Research Centre in which regular year-long symposia were organised starting in 1965-6, in areas in which the subject groups were strong and also in areas in which Zeeman considered UK mathematics required further development. In this respect, staff and graduate students were exposed to the world leaders in their subjects so that further research activities would occur.

In the Arts area of the University, a proposal was brought forward in June 1965 for a Centre for the Study of Social History. Here, it was considered that the Centre would bring about a new synthesis of disciplines, especially through the use of historical techniques to examine sociological problems. In particular, three areas were identified for study: social tensions during the transition to industrialism; urban growth and popular demoralisation; the social history of leisure. The main emphasis of the Centre was to be

upon research and graduate work – both features having a strong presence in the Centre in 1990. In the academic year 1990-1 Warwick has thirty-two centres, units and institutes that bring together research and predominantly postgraduate teaching in different ways. Some, like the original CIEBR, are interdisciplinary; others, like the Mathematics Research Centre, bring together members of a department with visiting staff from other institutions; and some, like the Centre for the Study of Social History, engage in research and postgraduate teaching. Together they have colonised the academic territory at Warwick alongside the departments.

Professor Christopher Zeeman, who founded the Mathematics Department and the Mathematics Research Centre at Warwick.

Conclusion

A dominant characteristic of the University has been the presence of strong departments which have engaged in teaching and research. For Jack Butterworth, the close inter-relationship between teaching and research was a key element of university life. This was well illustrated by his commentary for the university video in the mid-1970s when he stated:

> As Vice-Chancellor, I can tell you something about the unique character of a university and how it differs from every other institution of higher and further education. Here, you will undertake a three or four year course which will train you intellectually. Your mind, your intellect will be stretched by distinguished academic staff who are themselves working and researching at the limits of knowledge and because they will take you step by step to the very edge of the subject you are studying, you will be given the opportunity of improving your intellectual capacity. This is what a university is about and why it is unique.[63]

This statement reflects many of the key features of Warwick with research-led teaching in a relatively small number of strong departments that have been rated highly by external reviews, by research competitions and by students. For Warwick's single discipline departments with single and joint honours programmes have been a hallmark of the University and the undergraduate curriculum. Yet there have been many changes within subject areas with new programmes and greater specialisation. In turn, further specialist programmes have developed through graduate taught courses and research degrees. Similarly, the University's research activities through the work of individual scholars, research teams, and centres have developed and changed. Links with the locality and with industry have also become more systematic through a range of departments, including applied social studies, education, engineering, and industrial and business studies among many others.

Yet undergraduate programmes, advanced courses, post-graduate studies and research all come from the strong depart-mental base created by the founding professors. Indeed, when further subjects were added to the initial group, they were predominantly established by professorial staff who were given the opportunity to build up large departments. This was to have a further influence in the late 1970s when educational studies became an additional faculty. On reorganisation, the small departments in the former college were reconstructed in just four departments, thus mirroring the Warwick philosophy of a strong departmental structure. Such developments have been popular with students as Clark Brundin, the second Vice-Chancellor, remarked:

Students at Warwick generally attach a great value to the time they spent at the University . . . It's interesting to find how much they themselves feel they acquired from their time in the University, and also the very diverse ways in which they are using the training and the education that they have received at the University.[64]

Clearly, much is owed to the founding professors and their colleagues who not only developed their own subjects and constructed courses for students, but also contributed to the making of a university.

Acknowledgements

I am indebted to all those who agreed to be interviewed for this project, as well as many colleagues who checked information for me. In particular, Lord Butterworth made detailed comments on this chapter and provided additional information on early develop-ments at Warwick which I found very helpful. I am also grateful to Hilary Burgess, Ian Proctor, Rolph Schwarzenberger and Mike Shattock who provided comments on an earlier version of this chapter. Finally, I would like to thank Su Powell who has typed and re-typed this manuscript.

The University after Twenty-Five Years

To what extent has the University justified the ambitions of those who campaigned for it? If we look back to Bishop Gorton's paper to the Council for the Establishment of the University in 1954 (page 10) and to the debate in 1961-2 in the Executive Committee of the Promotion Committee about the proposed academic content of the University (page 19) we can see the extent to which the University's academic interests mirror the subjects then regarded as the most important. Thus Gorton, who of course was campaigning for a technological university, wanted technologies linked to the region, industrial relations and the study of business and public authority management. Industrialists, like the majority of those at the Barford House dinner in 1958 (page 14) and Lord Rootes and others on the Executive Committee, shared Gorton's view as to the importance of subjects related to manufacturing, particularly in relation to the automotive and aerospace industries, then the dominant industries in Coventry and its region.

In large measure these hopes seem to have been realised. Initially, the University was restricted to Engineering Science as originally agreed by the Academic Planning Board and as described on page 102 but, over the years the Department has greatly broadened its range while remaining a unified department encompassing all the major engineering disciplines. By 1990 its Manufacturing Systems Group had become the largest in Europe, and through a range of externally focussed programmes had developed a real partnership with major locally based manufacturing companies like Rover Group, Rolls-Royce and GEC as well as with many companies further afield. The Department as a whole covers a wide range of technologies and with over 1,000 students and a top UFC research rating it is a major resource for the region.

On the Business School side Warwick also seems to have made good progress. Because of the failure to secure support from the Franks' Report (see page 20) the University had to start the School on private resources. The first two professorships were funded externally, by Pressed Steel Fisher and the Institute of Directors. Undergraduate courses were not introduced till 1967. At that point the UGC was persuaded to make business studies eligible for UGC funding and since then the School has grown rapidly. The present School has 465 undergraduates. Entry to its undergraduate and postgraduate programmes are highly competed for and its research centres have high national reputations and have all undertaken research which connects strongly with the needs of the region. With the appointment of Professor Hugh Clegg, one of the School's earliest strengths was in industrial relations and the establishment of the Industrial Relations Research Unit in 1970 created what is generally regarded as the strongest research and postgraduate teaching group in Europe in this field. Like Engineering, the School was graded in the top rank in the UFC's research rankings.

Over this period the economic structure and the industrial mix of Coventry has changed very greatly. Of the companies represented at the Barford House dinner only GEC and Jaguar remain a major force in Coventry and most have disappeared altogether. The economic changes of the 1970s and 80s swept away a good part of the manufacturing base of the city and its region. An independent study of the University and its impact on the local economy stated that:

> Probably earlier than any other university in Britain, the authorities saw that the future of the institution was inextricably bound up with its relations with the outside world both through links with industry and through playing an innovative role in the local economy.[1]

In 1981 when the city was in the trough of the 1980s depression with unemployment rising above 17% the University and the City Council, in conjunction with the Warwickshire County Council and the West Midlands County Council, joined hands to set up the University of Warwick Science Park. The statistics of the success of the Science Park are described on page 80 but almost a more important contribution was to signal the diversification of the region's economy away from 'metal bashing' industries into the new advanced technologies. The success of Coventry's Westwood Business Park, which adjoins the Science Park, and the Warwickshire technology parks represents a fundamental shift in the industrial make-up of the region. The fact that the University took the lead in the Science Park, that its Engineering Department drew into the Park companies from the USA, France and Germany and that some of the University's academic staff and graduates, from biological sciences, chemistry, physics and computer science were among the first to establish companies there, is very much in line with Gorton's ideas and emphasises the extent to which the University has contributed to the introduction of new technologies into the region.

Of the subjects identified by the Academic Planning Board (page 20) all have done well. In its rankings in 1989, the UFC awarded grades for research from 5 at the top to 1 at the bottom. The Warwick 'score' from these subjects was mathematics 5, philosophy 4, politics 5, history 4, English 3, modern languages – French 5 and German 4, business studies 5, and biological sciences, which only began in 1969, 5. The overall aggregate (page 74) placed the University in fifth place in the *Financial Times* and *The Times* league tables. This was above any other of the New Universities and showed that in its first twenty-five years the University had overtaken many of the universities that when it was founded were regarded as leaders of the university system.

Gorton's belief in the value of a university also encompassed urban planning, social studies and the arts. The first was never developed at the University: a proposal for a School of Urban

Studies foundered in the early 1970s on the financial stringencies imposed on the University by the oil crisis. But in social studies the University has achieved national and international success with the Departments of Applied Social Studies, Economics, Law, Politics, Sociology and the Business School. The Department of Applied Social Studies, the Centre for Research in Ethnic Relations, the Institute for Employment Research, the Centre for Small and Medium Sized Enterprises and the Local Government Centre have all been active on research programmes within Coventry itself within the last three years.

In adult education, another of Gorton's concerns, the University has also been active. The University established a separate Department of Continuing Education in 1985 when responsibility for 'extra mural studies' for Coventry, Warwickshire and Solihull was transferred from Birmingham University. About 5,000 people a year now take part in the Open Studies (Warwick's title) programme in the three local authority areas. The Department has its own inner city task force based in Coventry and is responsible for 10 'access' courses to higher education run annually around the region. In 1990 the University had 1,400 part-time undergraduates and postgraduates, the great majority of whom were locally based. In Educational Studies the Faculty, created out of the merger with the Coventry College of Education in 1978, is responsible for an extensive in-service training programme for local teachers and about 60 Warwick graduates a year take teaching posts in the region. The Centre for Educational Development, Appraisal and Research (CEDAR) and the Centre for Education and Industry are both active in the locality.

Finally, both Gorton and subsequent supporters of the university idea believed that a university could introduce an important new cultural element into the region. This has been the major thrust of the Arts Centre which in 1989-90 attracted an audience of a quarter of a million people to its performances. According to a recent survey, about 30% of this number came from Coventry and a further 30% from Warwickshire and Solihull.[2] Comprising two theatres, a concert hall (the Butterworth Hall), an ensemble room, a film theatre, a gallery (the Mead Gallery) and a conference room, the Arts Centre is now the largest of its kind outside the Barbican in London and is regarded nationally as an important arts venue. The capital costs of building the Centre, spread over three separate phases, were covered partly out of the original Foundation Appeal, partly from contributions from the Nuffield Foundation (the conference room), the Arts Council (the gallery) and the West Midlands County Council (the concert hall), but the largest donations came from a resident of Kenilworth, Miss Helen Martin, whose father was Chairman of Daimler Cars in Coventry. Thus the community in its widest sense has continued to support significant aspects of the university idea which were focal arguments for creating a university.

But the founders always saw the University as also having a national and international impact. Measures of such an impact are hard to establish. At the research level the UGC/UFC's ratings in 1986 and 1989 establish the University as one of the leading national research universities, a standing which is reinforced by its thirty or so research centres, the presence of over 4,000 postgraduates and its external research income of £14.5m (1990). At the undergraduate level the University's reputation can be judged by its 20,000 home and over 1,000 overseas applications a year and the high qualifications of its intake. The growing public distinction of its graduates in all walks of life is a testimony to the University's standing. Internationally, many of its graduates hold high political, professional or academic positions, and one, Dr Les Valiant, won the 1986 Nevan Linna Prize, the equivalent in computer science of a Fields Medal in mathematics. The award of the Carl Bertelsmann Prize in 1990 marks a growing European reputation. The work of the Development Economics Research Centre in regard to third world economies, of the Manufacturing Systems Group in Hong Kong and Malaysia, and of the Education Faculty in Namibia, and the close relationships with major US universities, notably the University of Wisconsin at Madison, are examples of the extent to which the University has developed on the international scene.

It is no more than accurate, therefore, to say that the University can celebrate its first twenty-five years. The University's success reflects the far-sightedness of its founders, the Executive Committee of the Promotion Committee, the Academic Planning Board, the founding professors and, pre-eminently, the founding Vice-Chancellor. It has been reinforced by its ability from the Foundation Appeal onwards to generate external financial support. But it has also been dependent on the motivation and energy of its staff in a period of growing financial stringency and sharp reductions of UGC/UFC funding. Lord Radcliffe, the University's first Chancellor, in his installation address exhorted the University to be 'a brave University':

> I hope that it will be brave in confidence in its own opinions, brave in pursuit of its way, indifferent to those winds of vogue or fashion to which the world of education is much exposed, and that it will show its quality in a stern rejection of cliché and conventional phrase and an insistence upon probing through the surface of every problem, in whatever setting it may be presented.[3]

It would be an idle claim that Warwick, or indeed any modern university, has entirely lived up to this austere advice, but what Warwick has always been prepared to do is to take risks. These risks have tended to multiply in the 1980s but the University has continued to prosper. It is no longer reasonable to describe Warwick as a New University: it is a mature, well founded institution, academically strong and effectively managed. Twenty-five years is not, however, a point at which one can draw a line and conclude that its founders' ambitions have been satisfied. If there is a theme to this book it is that over a period of twenty-five years a university has been successfully established and is now ready to take on new challenges.

Footnotes and References

Making a University

1. Lord Cyril Radcliffe, "The University of Warwick", address delivered on installation as the first Chancellor, 1 July 1967, in *Not in Feather Beds, Some collected papers*, Hamish Hamilton, 1968, p.256.
2. A. E. Sloman, *A University in the Making*, BBC, 1964, p.9.
3. J. H. Newman, *The Idea of a University*, I. T. Kerr (Editor), Oxford, 1976, p.368.

The Pre-history of the University

CRO indicates a file held in the Coventry Record Office.
UGC indicates a UGC file held in the Public Record Office.
UWA indicates a file held in the University of Warwick Archive.

1. *Coventry Evening Telegraph*, 27 March 1943.
2. CRO 1/1.
3. UGC 1-2.
4. Lord President of the Council, *Scientific Manpower*, HMSO, 1946 (Barlow Report).
5. "Technological Training", *Financial Times*, 3 December 1951.
6. House of Lords, Science and Industry Debate, *Parliamentary Debates Lords* 1951-2, Vol. 177, 10 June – 17 July.
7. "Why not a University for Coventry", *Coventry Evening Standard*, 11 December 1953.
8. Letter by H. V. Field, *Coventry Evening Standard*, 26 January 1954.
9. Articles by Henry Rees, *Coventry Evening Standard*, 22 and 29 January 1954.
10. *Coventry Evening Standard*, 9 April 1954.
11. UWA PP/4/4, CRO 1/1 and 5/1 and W. H. Stokes Papers, Modern Records Centre, University of Warwick.
12. MSS 289 26 15, W. H. Stokes Papers, Modern Records Centre, University of Warwick.
13. CRO 5/1.
14. Richardson to Lord Mayor, 10 December 1955, CRO 1/1.
15. Report of the Council for the Establishment of a University, 18 April 1956, UWA PP 4/4.
16. UGC, *University Development Interim Report on the Years 1952-56*, Cmnd 79, HMSO, March 1957.
17. *Ibid*.
18. C. H. Shinn, *Paying the Piper. The Development of the University Grants Committee 1919-1946*, Falmer Press, 1986, p.96.
19. UGC *Interim Report 1952-56*.
20. Richardson to Secretary of the UGC, 23 February 1955, UGC 7/223.
21. Ministry of Education, *Technical Education*, Cmnd 9703, HMSO, April 1956.
22. Ministry of Education, *The Organisation of Technical Colleges*, Circular 305/56, June 1956.
23. UGC, *University Development 1957-62*, Cmnd 2267, HMSO, 1964.
24. D. J. Mitchell, *A History of Warwickshire County Council 1889-1989*, Warwickshire County Council, 1988, p.67.
25. See particularly Kenneth Richardson, *Twentieth Century Coventry*, City of Coventry, 1972, and George Hodgkinson, *Sent to Coventry*, Robert Maxwell & Co Ltd, 1970. I have also had the benefit of drawing on the unpublished diaries of Sir Charles Barratt and on the memories of J. Besserman, formerly City Secretary, K. B. Turner, formerly Associate Town Clerk and T. W. Gregory, formerly Chief Executive, Coventry City Council.
26. R. H. S. Crossman, *Introduction*, in George Hodgkinson, *Sent to Coventry*.
27. *Coventry Evening Standard*, 24 October 1958.
28. Notes of a meeting of members of the former Executive Committee of the Promotion Committee, 28 April 1965, UWA PP 4/5.
29. UWA PP 4/5.
30. Rees to Murray, 19 June 1958, UGC 7/223.
31. Rees to Murray, 2 October 1958, UGC 7/223.
32. H. Rees, *A University is Born*, Avalon Books, Coventry 1989, p.9; interview with Arthur Ling, 9 October 1990.
33. *Proposed University College in Coventry*, August 1958, UWA PP 4/4.
34. Barratt to Ling, 5 December 1958, CRO 1/1.
35. Ling to Barratt, 18 December 1958, CRO 1/1.
36. "Memorandum on the Creation of a University in Coventry" prepared by Walter Chinn for a meeting of the Coventry Education Committee, 17 October 1958, UWA PP 4/4.
37. Association of University Teachers, *Report on a Policy for Expansion*, May 1958.
38. *Coventry Evening Telegraph*, 3 December 1958.
39. Barratt to M. D. Webster, 21 March 1960, CRO 1/1.
40. Notes of a meeting of members of the former Executive Committee of the University Promotion Committee, 28 April 1965, UWA PP 4/5.
41. Taped interview with Sir Arnold Hall by K. E. Richardson: Audio Tape on Local History of Coventry, Coventry Polytechnic, UWA PP 4/1.
42. Henry Maddick to Charles Barratt, 19 December 1958, CRO 1/1.
43. Note by Sir Keith Murray, 7 January 1959, UGC 7/223.
44. A record of the meeting which took place on 27 April 1959 was made by Barratt (UWA Com EPC 1/1) but the account can be supplemented by a note by Chinn (CRO 1/1), by a brief account in Barratt's diaries (Vol. VI), from a letter by Chinn to Rees dated 29 April 1959 and from the taped interview with Sir Arnold Hall (UWA PP 4/1).
45. Note of the meeting held on 8 May 1959 compiled by Barratt UWA PP 4/4; note of the meeting compiled by the UGC, UGC 7/223.
46. Charles Barratt's diaries Vol. VI.
47. Henry Rees, *A University is Born*, p.29; Barratt diaries Vol. VI.
48. *Ibid*.
49. First *Report of the Vice-Chancellor to the Court*, University of Warwick, 17 November 1965.
50. *Ibid*.
51. Barratt diaries Vol. VI.
52. Barratt diaries Vol. VIII.

53. Minutes of New Universities Sub-Committee, 21 May 1959, UGC 7/169.
54. W. B. V. Balchin, "University expansion in Great Britain", *New Scientist*, 12 March 1959.
55. Minutes of New Universities Sub-Committee, 14 October 1959, UGC 7/169.
56. Murray to Barratt, 22 December, and Barratt to Murray, 29 December 1959, UGC 7/223.
57. Minutes of New Universities Sub-Committee, 28 January 1960, UGC 7/170.
58. *Ibid.*
59. Barratt diaries Vol. VI.
60. Correspondence between Chinn and Barratt, CRO 1/1.
61. This account is compiled from Barratt's diaries Vol. VI, from notes made by Henry Rees (UWA PP 4/3), and from correspondence held in the Coventry Record Office (CRO 1/1).
62. *Coventry Evening Standard*, 1 April 1960.
63. Taped interview with Sir Arnold Hall (UWA PP 4/1).
64. *Coventry Evening Standard*, 1 April 1960.
65. Barratt diaries Vol. VI.
66. P. J. Bennett to Barratt, 18 March 1960, CRO 1/1.
67. Richardson to Barratt, 31 March 1960, CRO 1/1.
68. Letts to Barratt, 21 March 1960, CRO 1/1.
69. Interview with Sir Charles Barratt, *Coventry Evening Telegraph*, 31 March 1965.
70. Undated note, Syers to Murray, UGC 7/223.
71. *The Times*, 16 June 1960.
72. Record of the visit to the UGC New Universities Sub-Committee, 16 June 1960, UGC 7/223.
73. Barratt diaries Vol. VI.
74. Record of the visit, 16 June 1960.
75. Letter from Syers to R. W. B. Clarke, HM Treasury, 31 January 1961, UGC 7/223.
76. Minutes of the meeting of the UGC New Universities Sub-Committee, 14 October 1959, UGC 7/169.
77. Evidence presented by the Incorporated Association of Headmasters at the meeting of the New Universities Sub-Committee on 28 January 1960, UGC 7/170.
78. Chinn, "Memorandum on the Creation of a University in Coventry", 17 October 1958, UWA PP 4/4.
79. UGC, *University Development 1957-62*, Cmnd 2267, HMSO, 1964, Chap IV.
80. UWA Com EPC 1/1.
81. Chinn to Principal of the City of Coventry Training College, 4 April 1960, UWA PP 4/4.
82. This account is based on the minutes and other papers of the Executive Committee of the Promotion Committee (UWA PP 4/4).
83. Quoted in a paper by Charles Barratt to the Executive Committee, 4 October 1960, UWA PP 4/4.
84. This account is based on the minutes and other papers of the Academic Planning Board (UWA Com APB 1/1), and E. T. Williams' private papers held by the University.
85. Report of Academic Planning Board to the UGC, February 1963, UWA Com APB 1/1.
86. Barratt diaries Vol. VII.
87. Hall to Williams, 7 June 1962, Williams' Private Papers.
88. The Franks Report, *British Business Schools*, 20 November 1963.
89. Report of Academic Planning Board to the UGC, February 1963.
90. Murray to Williams, 13 March 1963, Williams' Private Papers.
91. Paper by Chinn, 5 March 1964, UWA PP VC1 77-80.
92. Note of the meeting prepared by Weaver, 12 March 1964, UWA PP VC1 77-80.
93. Annual Report of the Principal 1984-5, Lanchester College of Technology. CRO SEC MB 113 1.
94. Note by Chinn of a meeting with Sir Herbert Andrew (Permanent Secretary, DES), T. R. Weaver, J. A. R. Pimlott at DES, 27 May 1964, UWA PP VC1 77-80.
95. Note by Chinn of meeting with Sir Edward Boyle, 10 June and with Sir Edward Boyle, Sir John Wolfendon and M. Dean on 26 June 1964, UWA PP VC1 77-80.
96. A. Crosland, Woolwich Speech, 27 April 1965, UWA PP VC1 77-80.
97. Note of a meeting prepared by DES between the Coventry LEA represented by Councillors Locksley and Lister, Chinn, Richmond and J. Besserman and the DES represented by Crosland, Lord Bowden, Weaver, Keggins, Melhuish and Coppleston (UGC), UWA PP VC1 77-80.
98. Taped Interview with Sir Arnold Hall (UWA PP 4/1).
99. Note of a meeting prepared by DES (UWA PP VC1 77-80).
100. UGC and University of Warwick, *Joint Study Group on the Role of Warwick in Technological Education*, November 1966, chaired by Dr F. A. Vick.

Illustrations:

Page 13: Model of a proposed University College in Coventry by Arthur Ling, Coventry City Architect and Planning Officer, published in *The Architects Journal*, December 1958.

Page 17: The University Promotion Committee visits the UGC, 1960.

The University Promotion Committee, from left: Dr Cuthbert Bardsley, Bishop of Coventry; Alderman B. H. Hunt, Chairman, Warwickshire County Council; Alderman W. Callow, Chairman, Coventry Education Committee; Mr Walter Chinn, Director of Education for Coventry; Alderman Harry Stanley, the Lord Mayor of Coventry; Sir Stanley Harley; Dr A. H. Marshall, Treasurer, Coventry City Council; Alderman Sidney Stringer, Chairman, Coventry Policy Advisory Committee; Mr Charles Barratt, Town Clerk, Coventry City Council; the Rev E. Lincoln Minshull; the Rt Rev Monsignor Canon Bernard Manion, Chairman of Birmingham Roman Catholic Diocesan Schools Commission; and Dr Henry Rees.

Page 19: The Executive Committee of the Promotion Committee, 1961.

The Executive Committee of the University Promotion Committee, from left, seated: Sir Arnold Hall (Deputy Chairman); Lord Rootes (Chairman); Mr Charles Barratt, Town Clerk, Coventry City Council; and Lord Iliffe. Standing: Alderman J. H. Steele, Chairman of the County Education Committee; Alderman B. H. Hunt, Chairman, Warwickshire County Council; Dr Geoffrey Templeman, Registrar of the University of Birmingham; the Rev E. Lincoln Minshull; Dr Henry Rees; Alderman Sidney Stringer, Chairman, Coventry Policy Advisory Committee; Rt Rev Monsignor Canon Bernard Manion, Chairman of Birmingham Roman Catholic Diocesan Schools Commission; Mr Walter Chinn, Director of Education for Coventry.

Page 21: Lord Rootes (standing centre) addresses those gathered for the launch of the Foundation Fund, held in the Institute of Directors Building, Belgrave Square on 9 April 1964. Lord Rootes is flanked by the Bishop of Coventry, Dr Cuthbert Bardsley (left) and the Vice-Chancellor, Mr J. B. Butterworth (now Lord Butterworth).

"Working and Researching at the Limits of Knowledge"

1. For a discussion of new university development see M. Beloff, *The Plateglass Universities*, Michael Joseph, 1968; H. Perkin, *New Universities in the United Kingdom*, OECD 1969; H. Perkin, 'The Last Virgin Births', *Times Higher Education Supplement*, No. 941, 16 November 1990, pp.13 and 17.
2. L. Robbins, *Higher Education*, HMSO, 1963 (The Robbins Report).
3. For a further discussion of developments in higher education see W. A. C. Stewart, *Higher Education in Post War Britain*, Macmillan, 1989.
4. A. Briggs, 'Drawing a New Map of Learning', in D. Daiches (ed.), *The Idea of a New University: An Experiment in Sussex*, Andre Deutsch, 1964, pp.60-80. However, many of the academic developments at Sussex were originally worked out by Lord Fulton (the first Vice-Chancellor).
5. The dominant characteristics of Sussex were well summarised in the graduate prospectus that states: 'Unlike most British universities, the basic organisational unit is the "School" rather than the department. Each School has its own courses at the undergraduate level which define its distinctive characteristics, and which are taken alongside those of the student's major; many majors can be taken in several different Schools. This means that there is a strongly inter-disciplinary atmosphere and many different kinds of cross-disciplinary link. Many growth points in research stem from these links'. *Graduate Programmes in Arts and Social Science 1991-1993, University of Sussex*, p.4.
6. A. E. Sloman, *A University in the Making*, BBC, 1964.
7. The data that are presented in this chapter have been collected through interview and documentary sources. The interviews took place in autumn 1990 and early 1991. All the interviews were tape-recorded. The interviews were 'conversations with a purpose' in the style adopted by ethnographers (for further details see R. G. Burgess, *In The Field: An Introduction to Field Research*, Unwin Hyman, 1984, and R. G. Burgess, 'Conversations with a Purpose? The Ethnographic Interview in Educational Research', in R. G. Burgess (ed.), *Conducting Qualitative Research*, JAI Press, 1988). The interviews were conducted with staff who had originally joined the university in 1965-6. The staff who were selected for interview included members of the original Board of Arts (subsequently Arts and Social Studies) and the Board of Science. They included four founding professors and members of the University who were appointed to each grade in the staff structure: professor, reader, senior lecturer, lecturer and assistant lecturer. They are: Professor Donald Charlton (founding Professor of French Studies), Professor Hugh Clegg (Pressed Steel Fisher Professor of Industrial Relations), Professor Alec Ford (originally appointed as Reader in Economic History), Professor Alastair Hennessy (originally appointed as Senior Lecturer in History), Professor Brian Houlden (Professor of Business Studies appointed from January 1966), Dr Michael Hughes (originally appointed as Lecturer in Engineering), Professor Terry Kemp (originally appointed as an Assistant Lecturer in Molecular Sciences), Professor A. Phillips-Griffiths (Griff) (founding Professor of Philosophy), Professor Graham Pyatt (Professor of Economics), Professor J. R. (Dick) Sargent (founding Professor of Economics), Professor Rolph Schwarzenberger (originally appointed Reader in Mathematics), Dr Tom Stone (originally appointed Assistant Lecturer in Molecular Sciences), Professor Christopher Zeeman (founding Professor of Mathematics). The data obtained from these interviews together with documentary evidence from newspapers, prospectuses, official reports to the University Court, minutes of meetings and committee papers have been used to portray key issues in the development of subjects, Schools, departments and associated university structures concerned with teaching and research. The chapter is written in the style of an ethnographic case study to reflect the words and work of members of the University of Warwick.
8. Extract from an interview with A. Phillips-Griffiths conducted on 23 October 1990.
9. Extract from Academic Planning Board Paper on Academic Standards and Courses, 1963.
10. *Ibid*.
11. *Ibid*.
12. *Vice-Chancellor's Report to Court 1967-68*, p.7.
13. *Vice-Chancellor's Report to Court 1969-70*, p.6.
14. In the UFC research selectivity exercise in 1989 Warwick was placed fifth in the ranking of universities.
15. D. Daiches (ed.), *The Idea of a New University: An Experiment in Sussex*, Andre Deutsch, 1964.
16. Extract from the Academic Planning Board Paper on Academic Standards and Courses, October 1963.
17. Extract from an interview with A. Phillips-Griffiths on 23 October 1990.
18. Based on a 'Note on a Common First Year Course', A. Phillips-Griffiths, 25 December 1963.
19. Extract from Memorandum on the Common First Year Course, A. Phillips-Griffiths, 12 January 1964.
20. *Ibid*.
21. *Ibid*.
22. *Ibid*.
23. *Ibid*.
24. *Ibid*.
25. *University of Warwick Prospectus 1965-66*, p.6.
26. Extract from an interview with Rolph Schwarzenberger on 22 October 1990.
27. Extract from an interview with Dick Sargent on 20 November 1990.
28. Extract from an interview with Christopher Zeeman on 13 November 1990.
29. Extract from an interview with Donald Charlton on 12 November 1990.
30. Extract from an interview with A. Phillips-Griffiths on 23 October 1990.
31. Reply to a questionnaire on 'History of University of Oxford',

November 1989, J. R. Sargent, copy of personal correspondence with investigators in Oxford.

32. J. R. Sargent, 'Are American Economists Better?', *Oxford Economic Papers* (New Series), Vol. 15, No. 1, 1963, p.5.

33. Extract from an interview with Graham Pyatt on 8 November 1990.

34. *Coventry Evening Telegraph*, 31 March 1965 – extract from a special supplement on the University of Warwick.

35. Extract from an interview with Alastair Hennessy on 17 January 1991.

36. Extract from an interview with Donald Charlton on 12 November 1990.

37. Extract from a paper entitled 'Some Notes on Engineering Science', J. A. Shercliff, January 1964.

38. *Ibid.*

39. In this respect, Arthur Shercliff was a pioneer as many science courses were only starting to consider women students in the 1980s. See J. Whyte, *Girls into Science and Technology*, Routledge & Kegan Paul, 1986.

40. Extract from an interview with Christopher Zeeman on 13 November 1990.

41. *Coventry Evening Telegraph*, 31 March 1965 – extract from special supplement on the University of Warwick.

42. *University of Warwick Prospectus 1965-66*, p.20.

43. *University of Warwick Graduate Prospectus 1966-67*, p.10.

44. Extract from an interview with Donald Charlton on 12 November 1990.

45. Extract from an interview with Graham Pyatt on 8 November 1990.

46. Extract from an interview with Christopher Zeeman on 13 November 1990. In this extract he comments on applied mathematics being part of his initial plan although some staff only recall this as being a view he held in the 1970s. When mathematics was established at Warwick it was based upon pure mathematics as applied mathematics was to be provided for in a range of other departments.

47. Extract from an interview with Rolph Schwarzenberger on 22 October 1990.

48. Extract from an interview with Michael Hughes on 14 January 1991.

49. *Coventry Evening Telegraph*, 31 March 1965, special supplement on the University of Warwick.

50. *University of Warwick Graduate Prospectus 1966-67*, p.23.

51. See G. Squires, *First Degree*, Open University Press, 1990.

52. Extract from an interview with A. Phillips-Griffiths on 23 October 1990.

53. Extract from a Report of the Joint Working Party of the Schools of Historical and Literary Studies, January 1970.

54. Extract from an interview with Alastair Hennessy on 17 January 1991.

55. *Ibid.*

56. Extract from an interview with Terry Kemp on 25 October 1990.

57. *University of Warwick Prospectus 1968-69*, p.71.

58. *University of Warwick Graduate Studies Prospectus in Science 1969-70*, p.36.

59. J. R. Sargent, 'Training the Future Leaders of Industry', *Coventry Evening Telegraph*, 31 March 1965.

60. Paper presented for Senate in March 1965 by Professors Clegg and Sargent entitled 'Industry as a Field of Study at the University of Warwick'.

61. *Ibid.*

62. Extract from an interview with Graham Pyatt on 8 November 1990.

63. Statement by Jack Butterworth on the University video in the mid-1970s and from which the title of this chapter is taken. Here, Jack Butterworth comments on research and teaching. However, he was also concerned that a university should be involved in service to the community – an idea he established through the teaching of Open Studies courses for the public (co-ordinated by the Department of Continuing Education), provision of teacher training (through merger with Coventry College of Education in 1978 which became a major component of the Faculty of Educational Studies) and the creation of the University Arts Centre that provides a range of programmes in drama, music and film for the general public as well as members of the university.

64. Statement by Clark Brundin on the University of Warwick video, 1989.

The University after Twenty-Five Years

1. Segal Quince Wicksteed, *Universities, Enterprise and Local Economic Development*, HMSO, 1988.

2. Survey prepared for the University by the Qualitative Unit, Millward Brown Market Research Ltd in June 1990.

3. Lord Radcliffe, "The University of Warwick", address delivered on installation as the first Chancellor, July 1967 in *Not in Feather Beds, Some collected papers*. Hamish Hamilton, 1968, p.261.

Notes to 'A Pictorial Account of the Development of the University'

Development

Title Page

The University site before building commenced. The College of Education buildings can be seen in the background.

Pages 26 and 27

1. The University Development Plan 1964, prepared by Arthur Ling and Alan Goodman. It will be noted that the Plan includes the 'Valley' relief road linking the A45 to the A46 which was never proceeded with.
2. The University Development Plan 1966, prepared by Yorke Rosenberg Mardall. This was the first Plan to include Warwickshire's gift of land in the University's planning.
3. University Development Plan 1972, prepared by Shepheard and Epstein.
4. The University campus at the end of 1990 showing the accretion of the Westwood campus after the merger with the Coventry College of Education, the development of the Science Park and the various 'design and build' projects of the 1980s.

Pages 28 and 29

1. The Library from the Molecular Sciences building, 1966 (Yorke Rosenberg Mardall).
2. The Molecular Sciences and Engineering Phase I buildings under construction, 1966 (Yorke Rosenberg Mardall).
3. The Library under construction, 1966. The exposed pipes stacked in the foreground are the heating mains which had to be replaced in 1987.
4. The Library under construction, 1966.
5. The Library and the Science Buildings from the area of Gibbet Hill Road, 1966.
6. The long walk between the Library and the Rootes Social Building, 1968.

Pages 30 and 31

1. Benefactors residence under construction, 1967 (Yorke Rosenberg Mardall).
2. Benefactors, 1969.
3. Benefactors, 1990.
4. Rootes A - C, Benefactors, and Rootes Social Building, 1967 (Yorke Rosenberg Mardall).
5. The Rootes residences from the Social Building, 1969.
6. *3B Series No. 1* by Bernard Schottlander, 1968.
7. Red Square, 1974.

Pages 32 and 33

1. The Rootes residences and Social Building prior to the construction of Rootes residences M - P, 1968.
2. View of the University campus, 1971.
3. The Air Hall, 1974. This was a Barracuda Air Dome put up in 1970 in the hope of providing a temporary solution to the lack of social space on the campus. It was not a success. By 1974 it was being used as a furniture store.
4. The Students' Union building, the banks and Whitefields residences under construction, 1974 (Alan Goodman).
5 and 6. The Students' Union building under construction and completed.

Pages 34 and 35

1. View over the buildings designed by Renton Howard Wood – the Senate House, the Chaplaincy and the first stage of the Arts Centre. Note the elm trees, which subsequently succumbed to Dutch Elm disease, in the Senate House courtyard.
2. The Senate House and Arts Centre stages 1 and 2 with *The Koan* by Lilian Lijn in place, 1976.
3. The Arts Centre theatre under construction, 1973 (Renton Howard Wood).
4. The Social Studies building first stage under construction, 1977 (Shepheard and Epstein).
5. Social Studies building, 1990 (Shepheard Epstein and Hunter).
6. Social Studies, 1990 (Shepheard Epstein and Hunter).

Pages 36 and 37

1. The central campus, 1977.
2. The Jack Martin residences, 1989 (Maxim Construction Ltd). These residences, providing 428 places with en suite bathrooms, are the latest residences to be built on the campus and were made possible by two substantial gifts from the Martin Trust. The residences are named after Jack Martin, the brother of Helen Martin, whose contribution to the University is described in more detail in the Appendix on the University Foundation Appeal.
3. The greening of the campus: plan of the new lake between the Rootes residences and Tocil Wood paid for mainly from the Parents Landscaping Appeal Fund.
4. View of the central campus showing Radcliffe House, the University's second post-experience training centre, 1988 (Phases I-IV: Clarke Construction, Phase V: Balfour Beatty Building Ltd).
5. The greening of the campus: view of the Students' Union building.

People

third Pro-Vice-Chancellor who was not a member).

3. Signing the Union building agreement: Nita Benn (née Bowes) on behalf of the Union and Professor Phillips-Griffiths on behalf of the Senate, 1974.
4. Secretaries Sheila Williams and Helen Lee (née Rudge) moving office furniture into the Senate House in 1972.
5. Jack Gowon, former President of Nigeria, who enrolled as a first year undergraduate student in Politics with International Studies in 1977. He graduated in 1980 and left the University in 1984 with a PhD.
6. The Vice-Chancellor and Phil Dixon, President of the Students' Union greeting Mr Fred Mulley, Secretary of State for Education and Science, on the steps of the Senate House, 1976.
7. Radio Warwick went on the air in 1971.

Pages 52 and 53

1. The Maths common room. Note Professor Christopher Zeeman's 'Catastrophe machine', top right.
2. Student styles in the mid-seventies.
3. Phil Mead, lay member of Council 1965 to 1983, Honorary Treasurer 1973 to 1983.
4. Students of the seventies: a well-used 'Prospectus photo'.
5. The musical tradition has always been very strong at Warwick: the University orchestra and choir conducted by Simon Halsey with Gaynor Keeble as soloist in the University Chorus and Orchestra's 21st anniversary concert in the Butterworth Hall, 1987.

Pages 54 and 55

1. A new Vice-Chancellor: Dr Clark Brundin on appointment to succeed Jack Butterworth, pictured outside the Sheldonian in Oxford, September 1984.
2. Freshers' weekend, 1987.
3. Registration, in the workroom, Rootes Social Building, 1987.
4. Post-finals student party in Economics, 1987.
5. Mature student about to graduate, 1987.

Pages 56 and 57

1. Sir Arthur Vick, Pro-Chancellor and Chairman of Council 1977 to 1990. (Sir Arthur remains Pro-Chancellor on retirement from the Chairmanship.)
2. Administrators and others in the SIBS case study room: from left to right Gwynneth Rigby (Senior Assistant Registrar, later married to George Bain – see below), David Palfreyman (Assistant Finance Officer, now Bursar and Fellow, New College, Oxford), Jonathan Nicholls (Administrative Assistant, now Senior Assistant Registrar), Pam Bate (secretary to Jim Rushton), Lin Fitzgerald (Lecturer, SIBS), Philip Moon (Lecturer, SIBS), Tony Rich (Administrative Assistant, now Senior Assistant Registrar, Sheffield), Steve Cannon (Administrative Assistant, now Financial Manager, Faculty of Medicine and Dentistry, Dundee), Ian Gow (Director, Japanese Business Policy Unit, SIBS, now Professor of Japanese, Stirling), Dr Roy Johnston (Senior Lecturer, SIBS), Jenny Hocking (Assistant Registrar, now Administrator, SIBS), Geoff Stevens (former SIBS Lecturer), Christine Laidler (former SIBS secretary).
3. Professor Gwynne Lewis appointed as Lecturer in 1967, now

Professor of History.

4. Professor Hilary Graham (Applied Social Studies), appointed in 1987.
5. Professor George Bain (appointed in 1970 to the Industrial Relations Research Unit), Chairman of the School of Industrial and Business Studies 1983 to 1989.
6. Professor John Tomlinson, Director of the Institute of Education, appointed 1985.
7. Professor Kumar Bhattacharyya, Professor of Manufacturing Systems in the Engineering Department, appointed 1981.
8. Professors in Biological Sciences: on the left, Professor Howard Dalton (appointed as Lecturer in 1975, now Professor) and on the right, Professor Roger Whittenbury, Chairman of Department since 1975 and currently Pro-Vice-Chancellor.
9. Lindsay Argent, Manageress and Clive Jones of the Entertainer Restaurant in the Arts Centre.
10. Professor Alec Ford (Professor of Economic History), Pro-Vice-Chancellor 1971-3 and 1977-89.
11. Mike Shattock (appointed Deputy Registrar 1969, became Registrar in 1983).
12. Jim Rushton (appointed Assistant Registrar 1969, became Deputy Registrar 1983).
13. Paul Bolton (appointed Senior Assistant Registrar 1973, became Academic Registrar 1984).
14. Colin Brummitt (Finance Officer since 1977).
15. Collin Ferguson (Estates Officer since 1973).

Page 58

1. Lord Scarman, Chancellor 1977 to 1989, photographed in front of the portrait by Tom Phillips which the University commissioned.
2. Sir Shridath ('Sonny') Ramphal, Chancellor from 1989, photographed as Secretary General of the Commonwealth in Marlborough House, Pall Mall, London.

Academic Work

Title Page

Student writing an essay in the Library.

Pages 60 and 61

1. Professor George Hunter reading in his room on the East Site.
2. Professor John Forty lecturing in one of the temporary laboratories on the East Site.
3. Professor Arthur Shercliff giving a tutorial in Engineering. He is demonstrating flow measurement.
4. PhD research student Dr Robin Felgett (writing on board), demonstrating a mathematical problem to Mathematics undergraduates in the Mathematics undergraduate common room, East Site.
5. Early Molecular Science Laboratory (Chemistry) on the East Site.
6. Dr Chris Alty (Engineering) demonstrating an N Flux Flow meter to a class.

Pages 62 and 63

1. Shift Leader Mrs Denise Dodd in the Computer Services machine room when it occupied the ground floor of what is now the Computer Science building.
2. Another view of the Computer Services machine room, this time from the operator's console. The Burroughts B6700 type can be clearly seen.
3. Computer Science students prepare punched cards for data entry.
4, 5, 6 and 7.   Students working in the Library. From the beginning it was planned that the Library should be the hub of the campus.
8. A demonstration of material from the Modern Records Centre in the Library. This is a major archive of modern historical materials mostly in the fields of labour and business history, trades unions records, the TUC archive and the archives of the CBI.

Pages 64 and 65

1. History of Art students outside the San Francesco della Vigna, Venice, 1988.
2. Film and Literature students using a Steenbeck film editing machine to view and analyse a film.
3. Roman set used in a number of productions (including the Roman play 'Pseudolus' by Plautus) standing in the Studio Theatre in the Arts Centre – a reconstruction created by Dr Richard Beecham, funded by the Nuffield Foundation, for a theatrical production by Theatre Studies students.
4. Classics students excavating an Iron Age pottery in Tocil Wood on the campus.
5. A Philosophy and Literature reading weekend in Wales. Staff members present include Christine Battersby (Philosophy) and Martin Warner (Philosophy).
6. History of Art students on the Rio della Madonna dell'Orto canal in Venice in 1988.

Pages 66 and 67

1. SIBS student Paul Taylor (later became a Research Fellow in IMRAD) at a lecture.
2. Dr Charles Jones, Senior Lecturer in International Studies, conducting a tutorial.
3. Mel Hirst, Senior Lecturer in SIBS, conducting a seminar on marketing with a group of postgraduate students.
4. A group of mature students in Sociology.
5. Sociology students in Leningrad with Dr Annie Phizacklea (Lecturer in Sociology).
6. Politics seminar conducted by John Halliday, Senior Lecturer in the Politics Department.

Pages 68 and 69

1. Students in Arts Education sketching at the Walker Shipyard, Newcastle-upon-Tyne under the supervision of Richard Yeomans (Lecturer in Arts Education), on right of the picture.
2. Science Education student Lorenzo Barratt in Chemistry teaching practice section in Alderman Callow School, Coventry.
3. Education student practising primary education in the practice schoolroom in the Department of Education.
4. Physics lecture by Professor Malcolm Cooper (first appointed as Lecturer in the Department in 1970).
5. Engineering student Lisa Moore with a computer controlled robot arm.
6. Computer Science lecture by Professor Mike Paterson (first appointed as a Lecturer in Computer Science in the Department in 1971).
7. Computer Science Laboratory.

Pages 70 and 71

1. Technician and student in Engineering casting precision aluminium components.
2. Engineering student Sarah Mann with fluid flow tank.
3. Computer assisted drawing office, Engineering.
4. Professor Muhammad Anwar, Director of the Centre for Research in Ethnic Relations (the national centre for work in this field) with some of the work published by the Centre.
5. A selection of publications by staff in the Faculties of Arts and Social Studies.
6. MA class in Women's Studies conducted by Dr Terry Lovell (Senior Lecturer in Sociology, seated centre), Chairman of the Graduate School.

Pages 72 and 73

1. Physics postgraduate Gary Heath with an early analytical scanning electron microscope, early 1970s.
2. Professor Mike Lewis (Physics, first appointed as Lecturer in 1967) with technician Gary Smith using an analytical scanning electron microscope, mid-1980s.
3. Professor Jeff Harrison (Statistics) giving supervision to research student, Mohammad Akram, now a Lecturer in Statistics in Bahrain.
4. Dr Vicky Lewis (Psychology) examining the reactions of babies and young children in the Child Development Laboratory, 1979.
5. Dr Keith Birkenshaw (Post-doctoral fellow), Dr David Hirst (Senior Lecturer in Chemistry) and PhD student Martin Jarrold (now with Bell Labs in the USA) with a crossed molecular beam apparatus used in the study of interactions between ions and molecules, mid-1970s.
6. Professor T. Saito (Tokyo), a visitor to a Mathematics Symposium on differential equations and dynamic systems in 1969 in the study of one of the specially designed Mathematics Research Centre houses.
7. Biological Sciences staff and student preparing sterile solutions in a sterile horizontal luminar flow cabinet.
8. Biological Sciences student preparing a fermenter in the microbiology laboratory.
9. Plants on a light bank in Biological Sciences' plant growth facility.
10. Biological Sciences student analysing a DNA sequencing gel.

Page 74

1. A chart published in the *Times Higher Education Supplement* on 3 October 1981, describing diagrammatically how the 1981 cuts affected universities in arts-based and science-based departments.

Warwick sustained an overall budgetary cut of 10% for the period 1981-4.

2. A table published in *The Times* on 21 May 1986 showing the allocation of UGC recurrent grant for 1986-7. Warwick with a 4% increase over 1985-6 received the highest increase of any university primarily because of the high research rating it received in the UGC's research selectivity exercise in 1986.

3. A league table published by the *Financial Times* on 26 August 1989, research selectivity exercise showing Warwick rated fifth in a national ranking of research.

4. Professor Terry Kemp, Pro-Vice-Chancellor and Chairman of the Academic Policy Committee, with the University's submission for the 1989 UFC research selectivity exercise. The UFC costed the exercise for the whole university system at £4m. The size of Warwick's submission tells you why.

5. Clark Brundin receiving the 1990 Carl Bertelsmann Prize in Gütersloh on behalf of the University from Herr Heinrich Mohn, Chairman of the Board of the Carl Bertelsmann Foundation.

Looking Outwards

Title Page

Display of books and monographs by staff in the Industrial Relations Research Unit.

Pages 76 and 77

1. The Electronic Nose team: from left to right, Dr Julian Gardner (Engineering), Dr Phil Bartlett (Chemistry), Dr Harold Shurmer (Engineering), Dr George Dodd (Chemistry). The project, which is being undertaken in collaboration with Bass plc and Neotronics Ltd, is to develop a monitor for aroma quality control of beverages and other products.

2. The Biotransformations group: from left to right, Dr David Hutchinson (Chemistry), Professor Howard Dalton (Biological Sciences), Professor David Crout (Chemistry). The Biotransformation Club was set up to collaborate with industry in the application of biological systems such as enzymes and microbes to the synthesis of chemical substances.

3. Nanotechnology project. Professor Keith Bowen (Engineering) (appointed Lecturer in 1968, became Professor in 1989), with an X-ray Interferometer Calibrator developed by the Centre for Microengineering and Metrology as part of its work in Nanotechnology. The Interferometer is now marketed by the Californian company VLSI Standards Inc.

4. Cancer Research. Dr Alan Morris (Biological Sciences) was appointed as a Research Fellow in 1976, Lecturer in 1979 and is now a Senior Lecturer. He holds a Fellowship (a career development award) from the Cancer Research Campaign. His research examines the reasons why cancer cells are not attacked by the body's own immune system.

5. The Advanced Technology Centre is part of the Engineering Department and was financed by the Rover Group and Rolls-Royce to undertake research in product and manufacturing technology and operational techniques.

6. The Centre was opened by the then Prime Minister, Mrs Margaret Thatcher, in 1990. She is here seen talking to Professor Bhattacharyya, the Director of the Centre, and Mr Hamid Mughal (Manager, LPS Conformance, Rover Group). On the far left of the picture is Mr Rahul Bajaj (Chairman of Bajaj Autos, India), and in the centre is Mr Andy Barr (Director of Operations, Rover Group).

7. Asea IRB-1000 automated assembly robot conducting dexterity tests. The robot is capable of moving at 2.5 metres per second.

8. Mr Mike Robinson (Chief Technician, Warwick Manufacturing Group) with an Automatix AI 32 robot carrying out welding on a Montego body frame. The robot was supplied by Automatix, a company on the Science Park.

Pages 78 and 79

1. The launch of the Science Park at the Press Centre in London. From left to right, Mr Antony Rudge, Regional Director of the Birmingham Office of Barclays Bank; the Vice-Chancellor, Jack Butterworth, and Sir Keith Joseph, Secretary of State for Education and Science. Barclays Bank invested £1.2m in the incubator building (the Barclays Venture Centre) which was the first building on the Science Park.

2. The site of the Science Park before the first investment, 1981.

3. The first buildings on the Science Park, 1984: the Barclays Venture Centre is the building nearest the University.

4. The Science Park in 1990. This picture shows the 18 acre expansion of the site from the initial 24 acres.

5. The Telemecanique building (Architects: The Edwin Hill Partnership).

6. One of the first tenants on the Science Park was Sinclair Vehicles. The company loaned a dozen C5 vehicles to the University. The Vice-Chancellor, the President of the Students' Union, Mike Moran, and the Registrar can be seen trying them out. It is not difficult to see why the company did not survive for long.

7. The West Midlands County Council Advanced Technology Unit: the second Science Park building, opened in December 1984.

8. The Barclays Venture Centre: the first building on the Science Park, opened by the then Prime Minister, Mrs Margaret Thatcher, in February 1984.

9. The DTI SMART Awards (Small Firm Merit Awards for Research and Activity), 1989. From left to right, Professor Graham Nudd (Computer Science) in respect to his company Warwick Strategic Technology, David Rowe (Director of the Science Park), Dr George Dodd (Chemistry) in respect to his company Osmotherapy, and Professor Roger Whittenbury (member of the Science Park Board).

Pages 80 and 81

1. Staff of Morton International, Dr Tim Lee (Technical Director) and Mrs Andrea Wilford (Project Leader) with Professor Terry Kemp (Chemistry) who was supervising Andrea Wilford's work on rubber reinforced epoxy resins for an MSc which she completed in 1989.

2. Dr Frank Grunfeld, who graduated in Engineering and Materials Science in 1978 and established a company, Nima Technology, on the Science Park in 1984.

3. Dr Crawford Dow (Biological Sciences), Managing Director of Microbial Systems Ltd, analysing a food sample.

4, 5, 6 and 7.   Statistics showing the growth of the Science Park.
8.   The London Contemporary Dance Theatre performing in the theatre in the Arts Centre, 1983.
9.   Musical opening to a summer conference in the Arts Centre, 1983.

Pages 82 and 83

1.   Simon Rattle and the CBSO in the Arts Centre.
2.   The 'Art From South Africa Exhibition', a touring exhibition organised by the Museum of Modern Art, Oxford, in the Mead Gallery, 1990.
3.   Riccardo Muti conducting the Philharmonia Orchestra in the Butterworth Hall at its opening in 1981.
4.   Simon Rattle conducting the Birmingham Symphony Orchestra in the Butterworth Hall.
5.   Terry Hands (Artistic Director of the RSC) and Trevor Nunn (former Artistic Director of the RSC) at the Golden Round exhibition, an exhibition related to the progress of the RSC Swan Theatre at Stratford, in the Mead Gallery, 1989. The exhibition was devised by Professor Ronnie Mulryne (English) and Dr Margaret Shewring (Theatre Studies).
6.   Peter Donohoe rehearsing on the Arts Centre's new Steinway piano, for the piano's inaugural piano concerto in the Butterworth Hall.
7.   Teaching children to swim in Westwood swimming pool.
8.   David Moorcroft of Coventry Godiva Harriers signing autographs on the University running track at a schools athletics meeting.
9.   A 'Sport for All' event in the Sports Centre in 1972. Paul Luxton, the world trampoline champion, and Jack Leonard, the US national tumbling champion, demonstrate various trampolining games.
10.   Children taking part in a Primary teaching practice session in the practice classroom in Westwood.
11.   Annual courses for sixth form girls to encourage them to study Mathematics at University are run by the Mathematics Department. Dr Rourke, Reader in Mathematics, is demonstrating a Mandelbrot set.

Pages 84 and 85

1.   Dr Nat Alcock (Chemistry) conducting a local history class in the Warwickshire County Record Office as part of the Open Studies programme.
2.   An Early Music Workshop in the Open Studies programme in 1986, with tutor Ian Harrison.
3.   The first graduating class of the Distance Learning MBA flanked on the left by Professor Robin Wensley, Chairman of SIBS, and on the right by Dr Roy Johnston, Director of the Distance Learning Programme. Back row from left: Professor Robin Wensley, Guy Fraser Simpson, Tony Hooper, John Venn, Toby Bencecry, Ed House, Mark Crompton, Bill Parsons, Tony Berry, Dr Roy Johnston (Director of the Distance Learning MBA Programme). Front row from left: Jonathan Dunier, Geoff Thomas, Gary Dardle, Roger Slater.
4.   Post-experience teaching in CAD/CAM in Engineering.
5.   The entrance to Radcliffe House, one of the University's centres for post-experience training.
6.   The annual Shakespeare Summer School for sixth formers run

jointly with the Royal Shakespeare Company.
7.   Chemistry Summer School for sixth formers.
8.   Schoolgirls on a Women into Science and Engineering (WISE) programme in Computer Science.
9.   The History Videos, a series of teaching videos made by the History Department for schools and further education colleges.
10.   Teacher Robin Hunter (left) on his six-month placement at Land Rover as part of the Advanced Diploma in Education and Industry. He is speaking to a colleague (middle) from the Range Rover Manufacturing Quality Taskforce. On the right is his supervisor, William Richardson, BP Senior Research Fellow, Centre for Education and Industry, Faculty of Educational Studies.

Pages 86 and 87

1.   Namibia. Dr Harvey Geingob, then Director of the United Nations Institute for Namibia (UNIN) in Lusaka, now Prime Minister of Namibia, signing an agreement with Clark Brundin, on behalf of the University. A group of Namibian students together with Jill Cottrell (Senior Lecturer in Law) and Mike Shattock (Registrar) are in the background.
2 and 3.   John Cunnington (Deputy Director, Institute of Education) and Mrs Thelma Henderson (Director of the Centre for English Language Teaching) who have led the University's relationship with Namibia.
4.   Mike Shattock and Peter Mauger at a meeting with officials of the Liaoning Institute of Education, Shenyang, Liaoning Province, China.
5.   The Overseas University Management Programme with Russell Moseley and Jonathan Nicholls (Senior Assistant Registrars) on far left and far right and Jim Rushton, Deputy Registrar, centre (seated).
6.   Ann Houghton, the administrator of the University's Hong Kong office.
7.   Professor Julian Gardner (Pro-Vice-Chancellor) with M. Jacques Delors, President of the European Community, signing an agreement in Brussels in 1988 setting up an integrated common law programme between Warwick and the Universities of Lille II and Saarland. Philip Britton (Senior Lecturer in Law), the architect of the agreement, is standing behind him.
8.   A Thanksgiving Dinner held by American students at Warwick, 1990.
9.   Simon Halsey conducting the University orchestra in a church converted into a concert hall in Palazzolo, Italy, as part of an overseas tour by the University choir and orchestra.
10.   The Festival of Languages has been held biennially at the University since 1986.

Pages 88 and 89

1.   The Lord Rootes Memorial Fund Awards were created from a fund raised by Rootes dealers to commemorate the death of Lord Rootes. The Awards support Warwick students in projects throughout the world. Pictured here is Engineering student Simon Browne (left) on an arctic survey expedition on which he was supported by a Lord Rootes Fund Award.

2. Engineering Design and Appropriate Technology (EDAT) student taking part in the installation of a novel pumping system in Zimbabwe.
3. Joint School of Classics student surveys the ancient Roman seaport of Amasra in northern Turkey.
4. Clark Brundin at the launch of the Malaysian branch of the Warwick Graduates Association in Kuala Lumpur with Christopher Thiagarajah, President of the Malaysian WGA.
5. Poetry reading by Continuing Education PhD student John Alford (centre) with Professor Fan Yue (Liaoning University) and Professor Yen Che Zhong (Shanghai Academy of Social Sciences).
6. The Queen opening the Physics building escorted by Professor John Forty and Professor Paul Butcher, 1970.
7. The former Prime Minister, Mrs Margaret Thatcher, looking at the development of frog embryos on a visit to Biological Sciences, 1984. Left to right: The Chancellor, Lord Scarman, Mr Denis Thatcher and Professor Hugh Woodland.
8. Michael Foot visiting the University to give a lecture on Byron as President of the Byron Society, 1989.
9. Prince Charles talking to members of the catering staff on a visit to the University, 1989.
10. Willy Brandt standing by the Cross of Nails in Coventry Cathedral after the award of an Honorary Degree in 1990.

Page 90

Professor Benoit Mandelbrot, mathematician, IBM Fellow, IBM Watson Research Centre, Yorktown Heights, New York, who in May 1990 visited the University to deliver a Public Lecture on 'Fractal Geometry, Nature and Chaos'; he is pictured here with a projection of part of his famous 'Mandelbrot Set'.

The following photographs are published by permission from: the Architects' Journal (page 13), Birmingham Post Studios (page 45:6), Director of Aerial Photography, University of Cambridge (page 36), the Coventry Evening Telegraph (pages 17, 19, 25, 33:3, 44:3, 46:3, 47:4 and 5, 48, 49:7, 50:1, 57:9, 76:1 and 2, 83:9, 88:5, 89:9), the Illustrated London News (pages 43, 44:1 and 2, 98, 109) and Times Newspapers Ltd (page 56:7).

We are also grateful for the use of photographs from the following sources: Aerofilms Ltd, Herts; British Leyland (Austin Morris Ltd), Cowley, Oxford; Susan Brown; Caters Photographic, Birmingham; Colin Davey, Camera Press Ltd, London; Jacky Chapman; H. R. Clayton Ltd, London; Commonwealth Secretariat; Cotterill Communications Ltd, Leamington Spa; John Barrington Cooke, Birmingham; Dales & Fleckner, Coventry; EEC Information Office, Brussels; Heart of England Newspapers Ltd; Dr P. Hills (History of Art); Haddon Davies Photography, Oxford; Junior Education Magazine; Ian Kerr; Keystone Press Agency Ltd, London; F. R. Logan Ltd, Birmingham; Agenzia S. Marco, Palazzolo; Roy McLeod; News Team, Birmingham; Dr Phizacklea (Sociology); Department of Physics Photographic Section; Daffyd Pritchard; Henk Smoek, London; Brian Sadler (Department of Economics); H. Tempest Ltd; Thomas Photos, Oxford; P. W. & L. Thompson, Coventry; University of Warwick Photographic Service; Alan J. Wood, Warley.

Appendix
The University Foundation Appeal

The Foundation Appeal was formally launched in April 1964 with a target of £4m, the highest target of any of the New Universities. The Appeal Working Party which worked under the umbrella of the Promotion Committee, comprised Lord Rootes (Chairman), Sir Arnold Hall (Deputy Chairman), Jack Butterworth (Vice-Chancellor), Sir Stanley Harley, Mr G. A. Hunt, Mr R. J. Kerr Muir, Lord Iliffe, Sir William Lyons, Sir Halford Reddish and Alderman B. H. Hunt, assisted by a fund-raising consultant Wells Organizations. There was absolutely no doubt, however, who supplied the main initial drive. In the *Case for the Establishment of a University of Warwick* submitted to the UGC in 1960 Lord Rootes had committed himself to raising £1m for the the first residences. By December 1964 he had personally raised £950,400 and his death in that month was to rob the University not only of its Chancellor-elect but of its most potent fundraiser.

The comparative success of Warwick's Appeal can be judged from an article in the *Financial Times* in January 1967 which showed Warwick having reached a figure of £2.75m as against Lancaster £2.2m, York £1.85m, East Anglia £1.4m, Essex £1.3m, Sussex £1m, and Kent £600,000. In October 1968 the Warwick figure was £2.857m. The breadth and depth of local giving gives an indication of the extent to which the community responded to the establishment of the University. The list of donors also represents a remarkable cross section of the industrial, commercial and private wealth contained in the West Midlands in the early 1960s.

The Fund was never, however, wound up and substantial donations to the University for specific projects have continued to be credited to the Fund. By 1990 the Fund had produced building projects for the University worth more than £11m. By far the most substantial donations came from a single source, the so-called Anonymous Benefactor, whose name was revealed after her death in 1988 as Miss Helen Martin, who lived at The Spring, Kenilworth. The full story of Helen Martin's benefactions to the University, and of the origins of her fortune in her brother Jack's sales of Smirnoff for his US company Heublein Inc, was told at the opening of the first of the Jack Martin residential blocks in 1988. The benefactions have been concentrated mainly on Anglo-American exchanges, through the Anglo-American Exchange Fund, student residences – Benefactors residence and contributions to the Jack Martin Hall complex – and to the arts, most notably £1.350m in capital grants to the Arts Centre and a continuous recurrent support towards music and the activities of the Mead Gallery. Helen Martin's contributions to the University represent one of the most generous examples of Anglo-American philanthropy towards higher education this century.

A full list of the donations up to 1968 is set out below. To appreciate the size of the donations at 1990 levels it is necessary to correct for inflation. The figure of £2.857m is equivalent to about £25m at 1990 prices.

List of Gifts

Donor		Total
Anonymous Benefactor/Miss Helen Martin		£360,000
Nuffield Foundation		£150,000
Ford Foundation		£104,600
Lord Rootes' Memorial Fund		£91,942
Chapel Fund:		
Founding Gifts	£70,000	
The Rt Rev Cuthbert Bardsley Bishop of Coventry	£7,000	
Wolfson Foundation	£7,000	
Banbury Buildings Ltd	£5,000	
National Farmers Union Mutual Ins Soc Ltd	£750	
Smaller Gifts	£2,075	£91,825
Alfred Herbert Ltd		£82,000
Automotive Products Ltd		£75,000
Bristol Siddeley Engines Ltd / Hawker Siddeley Ltd		£75,000
British Motor Corporation Ltd		£75,000
Courtaulds Ltd		£75,000

Donor	Total
Dunlop Ltd	£75,000
Guest, Keen and Nettlefolds Ltd	£75,000
Lord Iliffe (Coventry Evening Telegraph)	£75,000
Jaguar Cars Ltd	£75,000
Joseph Lucas Ltd	£75,000
Pressed Steel Ltd	£75,000
Rootes Group	£75,000
Warwickshire County Council	£67,419
Esmee Fairbairn Charitable Trust	£57,500
Barclays Bank	£52,500
Massey Ferguson Ltd	£50,000
Volkswagen Foundation	£44,280
Institute of Directors	£38,500
Rover Co Ltd	£37,500
General Electric Co Ltd	£35,000
Shell Mex and BP Ltd	£35,000
Coventry Corporation	£30,000
Leverhulme Trust	£27,000
Rugby Portland Cement	£25,000

List of Gifts (continued)

Donor	Total	Donor	Total
Tube Investments Ltd	£ 25,000	East Midlands Electricity Board	£ 2,500
Turner and Newall Ltd	£ 25,000	Edwards the Printers Ltd	£ 2,500
Unilever Ltd	£ 25,000	Gosford Press Ltd	£ 2,500
Imperial Chemical Industries Ltd	£ 21,200	International Computers and Tabulators Ltd	£ 2,500
Birmingham Small Arms Co Ltd	£ 20,000	Lloyds Bank Ltd	£ 2,500
Birmid Industries Ltd	£ 17,500	Midland Bank Ltd	£ 2,500
Sidney Flavel and Co Ltd	£ 16,952	National Provincial Bank Ltd	£ 2,500
Associated Engineering Co Ltd	£ 15,000	Radenite Batteries Ltd	£ 2,500
Rolls-Royce Ltd	£ 15,000	Valves Ltd	£ 2,500
National Association of Steel Stockholders	£ 14,000	West Midlands Gas Board	£ 2,500
Arthur Guinness Son and Co Ltd	£ 12,250	Westminster Bank Ltd	£ 2,500
ACLS	£ 10,750	Renolds Chains Ltd	£ 2,450
Triplex Holdings	£ 10,500	Minnesota 3M	£ 2,400
Courtaulds' Educational Trust	£ 10,000	Shell Research Association	£ 2,250
Coventry Gauge Ltd	£ 10,000	Cornercroft Ltd	£ 2,000
English Electric Ltd	£ 10,000	Goldsmiths Company	£ 2,000
J. & H. B. Jackson Ltd	£ 10,000	Solihull Borough Council	£ 2,000
Thomas Potterton Ltd	£ 10,000	Glynwed Tubes Ltd	£ 1,787
Prudential Assurance Co Ltd	£ 10,000	Iso Speedic Ltd	£ 1,751
Rubery Owen Ltd	£ 10,000	Rugby Advertiser	£ 1,750
Wickman Ltd	£ 10,000	Alcan (UK) Ltd	£ 1,750
'Local Authorities'	£ 9,125	Commercial Union Assurance Co Ltd	£ 1,750
W. H. Smith and Son Ltd	£ 8,476	Cathedral Garages	£ 1,702
Courier Press (Holdings) Ltd	£ 7,660	Cape Engineering Co Ltd	£ 1,702
Birmingham Post and Mail Ltd	£ 7,500	Alec Bennett Ltd	£ 1,695
The Bishop of Coventry	£ 7,000	J. & J. Cash Ltd	£ 1,695
Viscount Bearsted	£ 7,000	Reading Garage Co Ltd	£ 1,695
Simon Marks Charitable Trust	£ 7,000	Locke and England	£ 1,500
Cadbury Brothers Charitable Fund	£ 7,000	Regent Properties (Leamington) Ltd	£ 1,500
Vickers Ltd	£ 7,000	British Home Stores Ltd	£ 1,244
Albright and Wilson Ltd	£ 5,250	Ansells Brewery Ltd	£ 1,191
Unbrako Ltd	£ 5,157	Southerton, Martineau and Smith Ltd	£ 1,191
Smiths Motor Accessories Ltd	£ 5,005	Castles Motor Co	£ 1,185
Alvis Ltd	£ 5,000	West Midlands Engineering Employers' Association	£ 1,185
Bank of England	£ 5,000	Serck Ltd	£ 1,100
Coventry and District Co-operative Society	£ 5,000	Burgis and Colbourne Ltd	£ 1,050
Marks and Spencer Ltd	£ 5,000	John Straite and Sons	£ 1,043
Owen Owen Ltd	£ 5,000	J. T. Rhodes Ltd	£ 1,038
J. Arthur Rank Group Charities	£ 5,000	P. H. Woodward and Co Ltd	£ 1,038
H. A. Smith and Son Ltd	£ 5,000	Wright Hassall and Co	£ 1,034
Westminster Press Ltd	£ 5,000	George, Nelson Dale and Co Ltd	£ 1,021
Royal Society	£ 4,000	Benfords Ltd	£ 1,000
Parents' Landscaping Donations	£ 3,882	Coventry Motor Fittings Ltd	£ 1,000
Coal Tar Research Association	£ 3,644	Birmingham and Midland Omnibus Co Ltd	£ 1,000
Associated Portland Cement Manufacturers Ltd	£ 3,500	Dulverton Trust	£ 1,000
H. G. & T. W. H. Smith and Son Ltd	£ 3,404	E. Francis and Sons Ltd	£ 1,000
Associated Television Ltd	£ 3,257	Glass (Coventry) Ltd	£ 1,000
A. B. C. Television	£ 3,150	Improved Hinges (Warwick) Ltd	£ 1,000
Pilkington Brothers Ltd	£ 3,000	Industrial Mouldings (Warwick) Ltd	£ 1,000
Mills and Rockleys Ltd	£ 2,543	John Laing and Co Ltd	£ 1,000
Carter, Halls and Co Ltd	£ 2,500	National Coal Board	£ 1,000
Coventry Economic Building Society	£ 2,500	J. Rank Ltd	£ 1,000
Coventry Victor Motor Co Ltd	£ 2,500	Stuart Davis Ltd	£ 1,000

List of Gifts (continued)

Donor		Total	Donor		Total
Sutton Coldfield Charities Trust	£	1,000	R. Lloyd Ltd	£	525
A. Tomes Ltd	£	1,000	Alderman B. H. Hunt	£	511
Warwick Production Co Ltd	£	1,000	Murley Agricultural Supplies Ltd	£	511
R. S. Beard and Co Ltd	£	970	Burnside Investments Ltd	£	500
Carris Motors Ltd	£	851	St Halier Garage Ltd	£	500
A. Dyas Motors Ltd	£	851	Band Hatton and Co	£	500
Curry's Ltd	£	851	Baring Brothers Ltd	£	500
Halesbrigder Motors Ltd	£	851	Blythe Owen George and Co	£	500
W. S. Hattrell and Partners	£	851	Daffern and Co	£	500
Holmes and Son Ltd	£	851	Denys Hinton and Associates	£	500
The Motor Packing Co Ltd	£	851	District Bank	£	500
Chas B. Odell and Co	£	851	Harry Langford Ltd	£	500
Dr H. G. Hall	£	714	Lennon Brothers Ltd	£	500
John Harris Tools Ltd	£	700	George Loveitt and Sons	£	500
Sun Alliance Insurance Co Ltd	£	700	Martins Bank Ltd	£	500
R. F. Brookes Ltd	£	700	Mobil Oil Co Ltd	£	500
Tap and Die Corporation	£	700	Robinson, Osborne and Moules	£	500
West Midlands Engineering Employers' Association	£	700	R. A. Rotherham and Co	£	500
Brew Brothers Ltd	£	596	Hill Samuel and Co Ltd	£	500
W. W. Curtis Ltd	£	596	Wallwin Pumps Ltd	£	500
Davenport Vernon and Co.	£	596	*Smaller Gifts	£	18,331
Thomas Hunter Ltd	£	596	†Lord Lieutenant's Appeal to the Lieutenancy	£	5,871
R. M. Douglas Ltd	£	592			
Legal and General Insurance Co Ltd	£	592	**Total as of 4th October 1968**	**£2,857,104**	
Lazard Brothers Ltd	£	525			

Front Cover: *Aerial photograph (1964), showing the original University site with the present boundaries superimposed.*

Back Cover: *The roof of the Sculpture Court.*

ISBN 0 902683 14 4

Designed by Petrel & Porpoise Design, Coventry
Printed by William Caple & Company Ltd, Leicester